WriteTraits®
TEACHER'S GUIDE

Vicki Spandel

Grade 5

GReaT SøuRCe®
EDUCATION GROUP
A Houghton Mifflin Company

Vicki Spandel

Vicki Spandel was codirector of the original teacher team that developed the six-trait model and has designed instructional materials for all grade levels. She has written several books, including *Creating Writers—Linking Writing Assessment and Instruction* (Longman), and is a former language arts teacher, journalist, technical writer, consultant, and scoring director for dozens of state, county, and district writing assessments.

Cover: Illustration by Claude Martinot Design.

Design: The Mazer Corporation

Printed in the United States of America

International Standard Book Number: 0-669-49044-X

5 6 7 8 9 10 - BA - 07 06 05

Contents

Introduction

Unit 1: Ideas

Unit 2: Organization

Unit 3: Voice

Unit 4: Word Choice

Unit 5: Sentence Fluency

Unit 6: Conventions

Welcome to the World of Traits!

With the Write Traits® Classroom Kit, we offer you a way of teaching writing that helps students understand what good writing is and how to achieve it. The kit provides instruction in six traits of effective writing. The term *trait,* as it is used here, refers to a characteristic or quality that defines writing. The six traits of writing, as defined by teachers themselves, are these:

- Ideas
- Organization
- Voice
- Word Choice
- Sentence Fluency
- Conventions

Six-trait writing is based on the premise that students who become strong self-assessors become better writers and revisers, and we are quite certain that you will find this to be true. No matter where your student writers are right now, we are sure you will see improvements in their skills. You will also see them gain the confidence that comes from knowing writer's language and having options for revision.

Components in the Write Traits® Classroom Kit

Each *Write Traits® Classroom Kit* contains the following components:

Teacher's Guide
The Teacher's Guide takes you step-by-step through each part of the program, from introducing the traits to presenting lessons to wrap-up activities that bring all traits together. Also contained in the Teacher's Guide are 6-point and 5-point reproducible rubrics and sample papers to practice scoring.

Student Traitbook
Available as a copymaster within the kit or for purchase for every student, the Student Traitbook contains all the practice exercises for the six traits.

Posters
Hang the two posters for students to use as a handy reference when revising their writing.

Self-stick Note Pads (package of 5)
Use these handy self-stick notes to indicate your scoring and comments so that you won't have to write directly on students' papers.

Overhead Transparencies
Use the transparencies for whole-class scoring or for discussion of the sample papers in the back of the Teacher's Guide.

Writing Pockets
Available for purchase for every student, this writing folder serves as a reminder to students of the six traits and as a place to store their writing in progress.

Teaching the Traits units

The Teacher's Guide is organized into six units, one for each of the six traits. Each unit includes an overview, four lessons specifically designed to build strengths in that trait, and a unit wrap-up. At the end of the book are sample papers to use for practice in scoring papers.

Unit Overviews

Each of the six unit overviews accomplishes the following:

- defines the trait

- lists the instruction that will be emphasized

- provides a summary of each lesson

- contains two 6-point rubrics for scoring papers on the trait (one for the teacher, one for the student)

- recommends literature that can be used to model the trait

Traits Lessons

All twenty-four lessons, four for each of the six traits, follow the same format:

- Introduction, which includes an objective, skills focus, and suggested time frame

- Setting Up the Lesson, which introduces the main concepts of the lesson

- Teaching the Lesson, which provides teaching suggestions and answers for material in the Student Traitboook

- Extending the Lesson, which offers optional activities that carry the lesson concepts beyond the *Write Traits®* *Classroom Kit*

Unit Summaries

Each of the six unit summaries does the following:

• reviews the characteristics of the trait

• looks at the rubric

• applies the rubric to scoring sample papers

Warm-up and Wrap-up Activities

A warm-up activity is provided to help you introduce the concept of traits *("What is a trait?")* and the concept of analyzing writing by allowing students to assess right from the start. The warm-up activity helps students think like writers and heightens their awareness of the traits within writing samples. The wrap-up activities are designed to show you whether students have a full grasp of the traits and can use all six of them together.

Using Rubrics To Score Papers

Rubrics and Checklists

Please note that a checklist is NOT a rubric. The checklist included on your kit poster simply offers students a convenient way of reviewing their writing to be sure they have not forgotten any important elements of revision. The checklist includes no numbers and does not define performance at various levels along a rating scale. For this reason, neither you nor the students should use the checklist to assign scores.

Differences Between Rubrics

Our kit includes two 6-point rubrics for each trait, one for you and one for your students. We recognize that across the country, 4-, 5-, and 6-point scales are all in use. All have advantages. We believe, however, that the 6-point rubric reflects the greatest range of performance while still requiring raters to choose between generally strong papers (4s, 5s, or 6s) and papers in need of serious revision (1s, 2s, or 3s).

The 6-point scale allows the assigning of an "above expectations" score of 6. Further, it divides the midpoint portion of the scoring range into two scores: 3 and 4. Think of a score of 3 on a 6-point scale as a midrange performance, but one with a few more *weaknesses* than *strengths*. A score of 4, on the other hand, while also a midrange performance, has a few more *strengths* than *weaknesses.*

However, for your convenience we have also included 5-point rubrics, both teacher and student versions, in the appendix at the back of this Teacher's Guide.

Scoring Sample Papers

Sample papers included in this kit have been carefully selected to match precisely or very closely the grade level at which your students are writing. Some papers are informational; others are narrative. Some are well done; others reflect moderate to serious need for revision. These "in process" papers offer an excellent opportunity for students to practice revision skills on the work of others, and we recommend that you ask students to practice revising as many papers as time permits. This extended practice provides an excellent lead-in to the revision of their own work.

Suggested scores based on a 6-point rubric are provided for each paper. (Scores based on the 5-point rubric are in the appendix.) These scores are just that—*suggestions.* They reflect the thoughtful reading and assessment of trained teachers, but they should not be considered correct "answers." While no score is final, any score must be defensible, meaning that the scorer can defend it using the language of the rubric.

Frequently Asked Questions

How did this six-trait approach get started?

The *Write Traits® Classroom Kit* is based upon the six-trait model of writing instruction and assessment that teachers in the Beaverton, Oregon, School District developed in 1984. Because it has been so widely embraced by teachers at all grade levels, kindergarten through college, the model has since spread throughout the country—and much of the world. Traits themselves, of course, have been around as long as writing; writers have always needed intriguing ideas, good organization, a powerful voice, and so on. What is *new* is using consistent language with students to define writing at various levels of performance.

As a teacher, how can I make this program work for my students?

You can do several important things:

• Look to your students for answers; let them come up with their own ideas about what makes writing work, rather than simply giving them answers.

• Encourage students to be assessors and to verbalize their responses to many pieces of writing, including other students' work, professional writing, and your writing.

• Be a writer yourself, modeling steps within the writing process and encouraging students to use their increasing knowledge of the traits to coach you.

• Give students their own writing rubrics as you introduce each trait. Use the rubrics to assess writing and to help students see those rubrics as guides to revision.

• Share copies of rubrics with parents, too. This sharing encourages their involvement and helps them understand precisely how their children's writing is assessed.

Does six-trait instruction/assessment take the place of the writing process?

Absolutely not! The six-trait approach is meant to enhance and enrich a process-based approach to writing. Along with a wide set of options for revising, it gives students a language for talking and thinking like writers. Often students do not revise their writing thoroughly (or at all) because they have no idea what to do. Students who know the six traits have no difficulty thinking of ways to revise writing.

What do I do if I don't know a lot about the writing process?

Don't worry. We can help. First, you may wish to read the brief article by Jeff Hicks that summarizes the writing process. It appears on page xv of this Teacher's Guide and will give you all the basic information and terminology you need to work your way through the lessons without difficulty. If you would like to know more, refer to the Teacher Resources, page xviii. These resources will give you a strong background in the basics of the writing process, even if you've never been to a single workshop on the subject!

What do I have to give up from my current curriculum?

Nothing. If you are teaching writing through writers' workshops or any writing process-based approach, you will find that virtually everything you do is completely compatible with this program. It is ideally suited to process writing and particularly supports the steps of revision and editing.

Do I have to teach the traits in order?

We recommend that you teach both traits and lessons in the order presented because we use a sequential approach in which skills build on one another. Longer writing activities toward the end of each trait unit will require students to use the skills they have learned in studying a previous trait so that nothing is "lost." In other words, we do not want students to forget about *ideas* just because they move on to *organization*.

We do recognize, though, that most teachers prefer to teach conventions throughout the course of instruction, rather than as a separate unit. Therefore, incorporate instruction in conventions as you present the other traits.

Do all six traits ever come together?

Definitely. Writing should not be disjointed. We take it apart (into traits) to help students *master specific strategies for revision.* But eventually, we must put the slices of the pie back together. With this in mind, we provide several closure lessons, including one in which students will score a paper for all six traits and check their results with those of a partner. By this time, students will also be ready to assess and revise their own writing for all six traits. Wrap-up lessons may be assessed if you choose to do so.

Using Traits with the Writing Process

by Jeff Hicks

If writing were an act of fairytale magic or a matter of wishing, the word *process* would never apply to what people do when they write. All writers would have to do is wave their magic wands, rub their enchanted lamps to make their genies appear, or catch the one fish, from an ocean filled with fish, that grants wishes to the lucky person who hauls it in. *I'd like a bestseller about a pig and a spider who live on a farm. Allakazam! Presto! Newbery Medal!* Perhaps Roald Dahl was a fisherman and Beverly Cleary was a collector of antique lamps, right? Of course not! Writers understand that writing is a process involving multiple steps and plenty of time. An understanding of the process of writing is an important foundation for all young writers. Once they have the process in place, students can grasp and use the six traits of writing to help them revise and assess their own work. The six traits support the writing process.

The Writing Process The traditional view of the writing process is one that involves four or five steps or stages.

> **Prewriting**
> **Drafting (Writing)**
> **Revising**
> **Editing**
> **Publishing/Sharing**

1. **Prewriting**—This is the stage in which the writer attempts to find a topic, narrow it, and map out a plan. The writer usually isn't concerned with creating whole sentences or paragraphs at this point. Prewriting is done *before* the writer begins to write, and it is aimed at defining an idea and getting it rolling.

2. **Drafting** (Writing)—In this stage, the writer's idea begins to come to life. Sentences and paragraphs begin to take shape. The writer may experiment with different leads. In this stage, writers need to know that they can change directions, cross out words or sentences, and draw arrows to link details that are out of sequence. The term *rough draft*, or *first draft,* refers to writers in motion, changing directions and letting their ideas take shape.

3. **Revising**—When writers revise, their topics and ideas come into focus. In this stage, writers do a great deal of math—adding or subtracting single words, phrases, or entire paragraphs. What to revise often becomes clearer to students if they have had some time away from their drafts. Putting a draft away, out of sight and mind, for a few days or even more, may provide a sharper focus on weak areas. A writer might even ask, "Did I really write this?" The efforts made at revision will easily separate strong writing from weak writing.

4. **Editing**—This stage is all about making a piece of writing more accessible to readers. In this stage, writers fine-tune their work by focusing on correct punctuation, capitalization, grammar, usage, and paragraphing. Writers will want to be open to all the technological help (spell checker, for example) and human help they can find.

5. **Publishing/Sharing**—Not every piece of writing reaches this stage. The term *sharing* refers here to something more public than the kind of interactive sharing that should be happening at the previous stages. When writing is going to be "published" in the classroom or put on display as finished work, it needs to have been carefully selected as a piece of writing that has truly experienced all the other stages of the writing process.

These steps are often presented in classrooms as being separate, mutually exclusive events. *If I'm prewriting, I can't be revising. If I'm drafting, I can't be editing. If I'm revising, I can't be editing.* Mature writers know that the process may proceed through the steps in linear fashion, one at a time, but it is more likely that the parts of the process will intertwine. The process doesn't seem so overwhelming if a young writer can gain this perspective. I like to teach students several prewriting strategies—webbing, outlining, making word caches, drawing, and developing a list of questions—but I also like to show them through my own writing that prewriting and drafting can occur simultaneously. Having students experience their teacher as a writer is the most powerful way to demonstrate the importance of each stage and how it connects with the others. For instance, the best way for me to prewrite is to begin "writing." It is the act of writing (drafting) that often gets my ideas flowing better than if I tried to make a web of the idea. Writing also allows me to demonstrate that I can revise at any time. I can cross out a sentence, change a word, draw an arrow to place a sentence in a different paragraph, add a few words, or move a whole paragraph; all of this can be done while I draft an idea. At the same time, I might even notice that I need to fix the spelling of a word or add a period—that's editing!

Bringing in the Traits I know that many young writers speak and act as if they have magical pens or pencils. In the classroom, these are the students who proclaim, "I'm done!" minutes after beginning, or they are the ones who say, "But I like it the way it is!" when faced with a teacher's suggestion to tell a bit more or to make a few changes. Other students frequently complain, "I don't have anything to write about." Immersing these students in the writing process with a teacher who is also a writer is the clearest path to silencing these comments. Throw into this mix a strong understanding of the six traits of writing, and you are well on your way to creating passionate, self-assessing writers.

Teacher Resources

The "Must-Have" List for Teaching Writing Using the Six Traits

Ballenger, Bruce. 1993. *The Curious Researcher: A Guide to Writing Research Papers.* Needham Heights, MA: Allyn & Bacon.

Blake, Gary, and Robert W. Bly. 1993. *The Elements of Technical Writing.* New York: Macmillan.

Burdett, Lois. *Shakespeare Can Be Fun* (series). Willowdale, Ontario, and Buffalo, NY: Firefly Books.

Calkins, Lucy McCormick. 1994. *The Art of Teaching Writing.* 2nd ed. Portsmouth, NH: Heinemann.

Fletcher, Ralph, and Joann Portalupi. 1998. *Craft Lessons: Teaching Writing K–8.* Portland, Maine: Stenhouse Publishers.

Fox, Mem. 1993. *Radical Reflections: Passionate Opinions on Teaching, Learning, and Living.* New York: Harcourt Brace & Company.

Frank, Marjorie. 1995. *If You're Trying to Teach Kids How to Write . . . you've gotta have this book!* 2nd ed. Nashville: Incentive Publications, Inc.

Glynn, Carol. 2001. *Learning on Their Feet: A Sourcebook for Kinesthetic Learning Across the Curriculum K–8.* Shoreham, VT: Discover Writing Press.

Harvey, Stephanie. 1998. *Nonfiction Matters: Reading, Writing, and Research in Grades 3–8.* Portland, ME: Stenhouse Publishers.

Johnson, Bea. 1999. *Never Too Early to Write: Adventures in the K–1 Writing Workshop.* Gainesville, FL: Maupin House Publishing.

Kemper, Dave, et al. 2000. *Writers Express: A Handbook for Young Writers, Thinkers, and Learners.* Wilmington, MA: Great Source Education Group, Inc.

Lamott, Anne. 1994. *Bird by Bird: Some Instructions on Writing and Life.* New York: Doubleday.

Lane, Barry. 1998. *The Reviser's Toolbox.* Shoreham, VT: Discover Writing Press.

Murray, Donald M. 1985. *A Writer Teaches Writing.* 2nd ed. New York: Houghton Mifflin.

O'Conner, Patricia T. 1999. *Words Fail Me: What Everyone Who Writes Should Know About Writing.* New York: Harcourt Brace & Company.

Portalupi, Joann, with Ralph Fletcher. 2001. *Nonfiction Craft Lessons: Teaching Information Writing K–8.* Portland, Maine: Stenhouse Publishers.

Spandel, Vicki. 2001. *Creating Writers.* 3rd ed. New York: Allyn & Bacon.

Spandel, Vicki, with Ruth Nathan and Laura Robb. 2001. *Daybook of Critical Reading and Writing.* (Grade 5). Wilmington, MA: Great Source Education Group, Inc.

Stiggins, Richard J. 1996. *Student-Centered Classroom Assessment.* 2nd ed. Columbus, OH: Prentice Hall (Merrill).

Thomason, Tommy. 1998. *Writer to Writer: How to Conference Young Authors.* Norwood, MA: Christopher Gordon Publishers.

Thomason, Tommy, and Carol York. 2000. *Write on Target: Preparing Young Writers to Succeed on State Writing Achievement Tests.* Norwood, MA: Christopher Gordon Publishers.

Using Write Traits Classroom Kits
with *Writers Express*©

Write Traits Classroom Kit, Grade 5	Skill Focus	*Writers Express* (Copyright© 2000)
Unit 1: Ideas		
Lesson 1: Taming the Wild Topic	Narrow the topic	Activities for choosing a subject, p. 36
Lesson 2: Targeted Writing	Stay focused on the topic	The Parts of a Paragraph, p. 76
Lesson 3: Details on a Diet	Choose interesting details	Organize Your Details, p. 48
Lesson 4: Filling in the Details	Include the details a reader needs	Adding Details, p. 83
Unit 2: Organization		
Lesson 5: Take Me to Your *Lead*-er	Write a strong lead	Writing a Lead, p. 163
Lesson 6: That's an Order!	Order the information logically	Putting Things in Order, p. 84
Lesson 7: Sticking with It	Stick with the main idea	Develop a Writing Plan, p. 47
Lesson 8: Beware, the End Is Near!	Write a strong conclusion	Writing the Ending, p. 53
Unit 3: Voice		
Lesson 9: Matching Voice and Purpose	Match the voice to the purpose	Writing a Descriptive Essay (Voice), p. 101
Lesson 10: Raising Your Voice	Revise to make voice stronger	Checklist for Good Writing, p. 23
Lesson 11: All-Star Voices	Imitate a favorite voice	Personal Voice, p. 21
Lesson 12: It's All About You	Write with a strong voice	Writing Personal Narratives, pp. 138–143

Unit 4: Word Choice		
Lesson 13: Lights, Camera, Action!	Use strong verbs	Vivid Verbs, p. 127
Lesson 14: Headline News —Use Writer's Clues!	Use context to learn words	Building Vocabulary Skills, pp. 288–294
Lesson 15: Painting Word Pictures	Use sensory language	Checking for Word Choice, p. 66
Lesson 16: Brush Strokes, Not Buckets!	Cut out unnecessary words	Revising Checklist, p. 57
Unit 5: Sentence Fluency		
Lesson 17: Rolling Like a River	Combine sentences	Combining Sentences, pp. 118–121
Lesson 18: VARY Length— or Be VERY Boring!	Vary sentence length	Checking for Smooth Sentences, p. 65
Lesson 19: Dynamite Dialogue	Use dialogue	Writing Dialogue, p. 215
Lesson 20: Focusing on Fluency in Your Own Writing	Revise for fluency	Editing and Proofreading, p. 16
Unit 6: Conventions		
Lesson 21: Burgers, Granola Bars, Revising, and Editing	Define revising and editing	Revising and Editing, pp. 54–67
Lesson 22: Developing Your Editor's Eye	Find errors	Editing and Proofreading Checklist, p. 67
Lesson 23: Clang the Symbols!	Use editor's marks	Editing and Proofreading Marks, p. 441
Lesson 24: Editing Is the Name of the Game	Edit text	Editing and Proofreading, p. 16

Write Traits® Classroom Kit
SCOPE AND SEQUENCE

Trait/Skill	Grade 3	4	5	6	7	8
IDEAS						
Narrowing the Topic			•	•	•	•
Getting Started	•	•		•		•
Identifying the Main Idea	•	•	•			
Clarifying Ideas				•	•	•
Expanding Sketchy Writing			•	•	•	
Identifying What Is Important	•	•	•			
Making Writing Concise	•	•			•	•
ORGANIZATION						
Writing a Strong Lead	•	•	•			
Putting Things in Order	•		•		•	
Identifying Organizational Patterns		•		•		•
Matching Organizational Pattern and Writing Task		•		•		•
Staying on Topic	•		•		•	
Creating Strong Transitions				•	•	•
Writing Endings	•	•	•			
Putting Details Together				•	•	•
VOICE						
Defining Voice				•	•	•
Matching Voice and Purpose	•		•		•	
Putting Voice into Personal Narrative	•	•	•			
Putting Voice into Expository Writing				•	•	•
Matching Voice to Audience				•	•	•
Sharing Favorite Voices	•	•	•			
Putting Voice into Flat Writing		•		•		•
Using Personal Voice	•	•	•			

Trait/Skill	Grade					
	3	4	5	6	7	8
WORD CHOICE						
Using Strong Verbs	•	•	•			
Using Synonyms and Antonyms to Enhance Meaning				•	•	•
Inferring Meaning from Context	•	•	•			
Using Sensory Words to Create a Word Picture	•	•	•	•		•
Using Strong Words to Revise Flat Writing				•	•	•
Revising Overwritten Language		•		•	•	•
Eliminating Wordiness	•		•		•	
SENTENCE FLUENCY						
Making Choppy Writing Fluent	•		•		•	
Varying Sentence Beginnings	•	•				•
Varying Sentence Length			•	•	•	
Eliminating Run-ons	•	•		•		
Inserting Transitions				•	•	•
Creating Dialogue	•	•	•			
Assessing Fluency Through Interpretive Reading		•		•		•
Reading and Revising Personal Text			•		•	•
CONVENTIONS						
Distinguishing Between Revision and Editing		•	•	•	•	•
Spotting Errors	•		•		•	
Knowing the Symbols	•	•	•	•	•	•
Correcting Errors	•	•	•	•	•	•
Creating an Editing Checklist	•	•		•		•

Warm-up Activity

The warm-up activity is designed to help students assess writing for strengths and weaknesses. Students do not need to be familiar with the six traits to do this exercise. However, you may wish to introduce the activity by defining *trait* as "a characteristic or quality that helps define any concept." Encourage students to brainstorm the traits of something with which they are familiar, such as a book or a game. This activity can be a warm-up for discussing the traits of good writing and will help students understand what a trait is. The activity should take about 35 minutes.

Ranking Three Papers

For use with Student Traitbook pages 5–6

This extended warm-up activity will help students begin working as assessors and thinking about what makes a piece of writing strong or weak. Students will not score these samples but will rank them from strongest to weakest and discuss their differences. In the discussions, you will probably hear the language of the traits even if you have not introduced them.

Students will read three versions of the writer's encounter with an aggressive dog named Bristles on pages 5–6 in the Student Traitbook. The descriptions differ in quality and extent of detail, completeness of organizational structure, word choice, and voice. Conventions are quite strong in *all* examples because the purpose of the activity is to get students to think beyond conventions to the other elements that make writing work.

Tell students to make marks on the paragraphs as you read aloud or as they read silently. Suggest that students circle or underline those parts that stand out because they are weak or strong. After reading or listening to each paragraph, students should use their marks to help them decide which paragraph is the strongest and which is the weakest. They should give reasons for ranking the papers in a particular way.

Ask students to share their rankings (record these on an overhead) and to explain their reasons briefly.

Rationales for Ranking

Students should see Sample 2 as the strongest. It has an excellent lead and conclusion and is well organized. Rich details make the event easy for the reader to picture. The writer uses enthusiasm and humor to project strong voice, and the word choice is lively. The writer also remains focused throughout, never losing sight of the main story. The piece is fluent, too, because of variety in sentence length and structure.

Sample 3 lacks the detail of Sample 2, but it does provide a fairly clear picture of events and it never loses focus. The voice is not as energetic or as humorous as the voice in Sample 2, but it does have a moderate amount of voice. Word choice is strong, and sentences are well constructed. The organization is solid, though not especially creative. The lead is not nearly as strong as that in Sample 2, but the conclusion works well.

Sample 1 is certainly the most in need of revision. It has several problems. First, it lacks focus. Details seem random, and many are unnecessary. (Does it matter whether Brad went to the dentist or whether the writer will one day be a lifeguard?) Sample 1 is not especially fluent, and sentences tend to be similar in length; too many begin with *I*. Word choice and voice are adequate but not striking. This writer sounds a little bored.

Extensions

- Discuss what students can do to revise any of the three writing samples.

- Ask students to select one of the weaker samples (Sample 1 or Sample 3) and to revise it, using any details they like. Allow students to invent or delete information if they wish to do so.

- Ask each student to write a brief paragraph describing an encounter—good or bad—with an animal of any kind. These paragraphs should be well detailed, modeling Sample 2. Share some paragraphs aloud.

- Make a chart of **Strengths** and **Problems.** List all of the strengths and problems students notice for each of the three papers. Compare the lists. Do they show that students have ranked the papers appropriately?

WriteTraits®

Unit 1
Ideas

Overview

This unit focuses on the concept of ideas—the writer's main message and all the details that support it. Students will practice identifying main ideas, selecting a manageable topic, selecting important and relevant details that support a main idea, and filling in "holes" to add missing information. The purpose of this unit is to help students create "balanced" writing—writing with sufficient detail to be both clear and interesting, yet not so loaded with unnecessary information that the reader feels overwhelmed.

The focus of the instruction in this unit will be

- guiding students to choose a topic and write clearly about that topic
- showing students how to use prewriting strategies that help bring focus to their writing
- modeling the difference between details everyone knows and special details that make writing interesting
- reminding students to include details that support the main idea

Ideas: *A Definition*

Ideas are all about information. In a strong creative piece, ideas paint a picture in the reader's mind. In an informational piece, strong ideas make difficult or complex information easy to understand. Good writing always makes sense. It always has a message, main point, or story to tell. And it always includes details—not just any details, but those beyond-the-obvious bits of information that thoughtful, observant writers notice.

The Unit at a Glance

The following lessons in the Teacher's Guide and practice exercises in the Student Traitbook will help develop understanding of the trait of ideas. The Unit Summary provides an opportunity to practice evaluating papers for ideas.

Unit Introduction: Ideas

Teacher's Guide pages 2–6
Student Traitbook page 7

Students are introduced to the trait of ideas.

Lesson 1: Taming the Wild Topic

Teacher's Guide pages 7–9
Student Traitbook pages 8–11

Students learn to take a broad topic and narrow it down to manageable size.

Lesson 2: Targeted Writing

Teacher's Guide pages 10–12
Student Traitbook pages 12–15

Students practice identifying a main point and recognizing writing that has no main point. Students also learn how to use a simple prewriting strategy to make the main point the focus of the writing.

Lesson 3: Details on a Diet

Teacher's Guide pages 13–15
Student Traitbook pages 16–19

Students learn to be selective in choosing details that support a main idea.

Lesson 4: Filling in the Details

Teacher's Guide pages 16–18
Student Traitbook pages 20–23

Students learn to spot "holes" in their writing and fill them with needed information.

Unit Summary: Ideas

Teacher's Guide page 19
Overhead numbers 1–4

Use the rubric on page 5 and the activities in the Summary to practice evaluating writing for ideas, details, and clarity.

Teacher Rubric for Ideas

6 ▪ The main idea of the paper is clear. The message or story is interesting—even memorable.
  ▪ The writer seems to have in-depth understanding of or insight about the topic, message, characters, and so on.
  ▪ The writer is selective, including details that hold a reader's attention throughout the piece.

5 ▪ This paper makes sense from beginning to end. It is clear—never confusing.
  ▪ The writer knows enough about the topic to do a thorough job.
  ▪ The paper contains many interesting details.

4 ▪ The reader can identify the writer's main idea.
  ▪ The writer has some knowledge of the topic; more would enrich the paper.
  ▪ The writing includes some interesting or unusual details—enough to make the reader wish for more.

3 ▪ It is fairly easy to identify the main idea. Some details are unclear, however, or do not seem to enhance the main idea or story.
  ▪ Sometimes the writer appears to know what he or she is talking about; at other times, the writer seems to search for things to say.
  ▪ Detail is present but minimal. Much of the writing consists of general statements that do little to expand the main message.

2 ▪ The main idea or story is hard to determine. The paper lacks clarity.
  ▪ The writer does not appear to have a clear message or know much about this topic, and writes mainly to fill space.
  ▪ Details are sketchy or absent. The paper simply does not say much.

1 ▪ This writer has no main idea or story. The writing consists mainly of random thoughts or notes.
  ▪ The reader cannot extract anything meaningful.
  ▪ It is all but impossible to summarize this writing.

Student Rubric for Ideas

6
- The main idea of my paper is clear. It is easy to understand what I mean.
- I know a lot about this topic.
- My paper is full of interesting, unusual details that will keep readers reading.

5
- This paper makes sense. The main idea is clear.
- I know quite a bit about this topic.
- My paper contains many interesting details.

4
- The reader can identify my main idea.
- I know some things about this topic. I wish I knew more.
- My paper has some interesting details. It could use more.

3
- The reader can probably guess what my main idea is. Some parts of the paper are not clear.
- I need more information. Sometimes I guessed or made things up.
- There is not much detail. The paper is mostly general statements.

2
- My main idea is hard to figure out. The reader may wonder what I am trying to say.
- I do not know much about this topic. I wrote to fill space.
- I need a lot more detail. This paper does not tell much.

1
- I do not have a main idea. I wrote whatever came into my head.
- I'm not sure what I want to say.
- None of this is clear. The reader will wonder what point I am trying to make.

Recommended Literature for Teaching Ideas

This list of recommended books is a resource; use the books that are part of your usual curriculum if you prefer. Ask students to listen for details or for main ideas and then to comment on details they recall or to pose questions about anything the author has not made clear.

Bartoletti, Susan Campbell. 1996. *Growing Up in Coal Country.* Boston: Houghton Mifflin. This is a detailed nonfiction account of children working as coal miners.

Cleary, Beverly. 1988. *A Girl From Yamhill.* New York: William Morrow and Company, Inc. This memoir provides intriguing detail on every page.

Collard, Sneed B. III. 1996. *Alien Invaders: The Continuing Threat of Exotic Species.* Danbury, CT: Franklin Watts. This book has strong main themes with vivid details of plants and animals relocating—often where they're not wanted.

DiCamillo, Kate. 2000. *Because of Winn-Dixie.* Cambridge, MA: Candlewick Press. The simple but eloquent prose provides excellent descriptions and characterization.

Kemper, Dave, with Ruth Nathan, Patrick Sebranek, and Carol Elsholz. 2000. *Writers Express: A Handbook for Young Writers, Thinkers, and Learners.* Wilmington, MA: Great Source. Using details, forming a main idea, staying on topic—here are all the basics you need to bring the trait of ideas to life.

Krull, Kathleen. 1994. *Lives of the Writers: Comedies, Tragedies, and What the Neighbors Thought.* San Diego: Harcourt Brace & Company. This selection answers the questions you would ask of famous writers if you could do an interview.

Macaulay, David. 1998. *The New Way Things Work.* Boston: Houghton Mifflin. This book shows how details clarify informational or technical writing.

Price, Reynolds. 2000. *A Perfect Friend.* New York: Atheneum Books for Young Readers. Two strong main ideas are thoughtfully explored here: Overcoming grief and bonding with a very special animal.

Roberts, Willo Davis. 2001. *Buddy Is a Stupid Name for a Girl.* New York: Atheneum Books for Young Readers. The main idea here—Buddy's search for her father and for the truth—keeps everything else in focus. It is also an excellent choice for illustrating voice.

Spandel, Vicki, with Ruth Nathan and Laura Robb. 2001. *Daybook of Critical Reading and Writing* (Grade 5 edition). Wilmington, MA: Great Source. This is a marvelous collage of reading and writing activities based on the most exceptional literature of our time.

Taming the Wild Topic

For use with pages 7–11 in the Student Traitbook

In this lesson, students learn the importance of narrowing a topic to a manageable size. Broad topics are awkward and often lead to writing sprawl that is full of generalities.

Objectives

Students will learn a specific strategy to make a large topic more manageable.

Skills Focus

- Recognizing the difference between too broad a topic and one that is narrow enough to manage easily
- Asking the right questions to help narrow a topic
- Working with a partner to "funnel" a topic down to size
- Working independently to "funnel" a topic down to size

Time Frame

Allow about 40 minutes for this lesson. It can be divided into two parts. Ask students to review the example on "Taming Animals," and then to work with a partner on taming the topic "Fish" (20 minutes). In part 2 of the lesson, ask students to select a topic (under "You Are the Tamer"), to narrow it by "pushing it through the funnel," and then to assess their funneling skills (20 minutes).

Setting Up the Lesson

Use the introduction on Student Traitbook page 7 to present the trait of ideas. Give students some practice in "funneling" and in asking good questions by providing a large topic of your own and asking for their help in narrowing it down. Possible large topics might include these:

- School
- Television
- Weather
- Travel
- Food

Choose one of these topics or a topic of your own, and have students ask *Who, What, When, Where, Why, How, Which,* and *Is* questions until the topic is small enough to write about. You may wish to write a line or two to show students that it is easier to begin writing when the topic is narrow. Model narrowing more than one topic if students need more practice.

Teaching the Lesson

Pushing It Through the Funnel

Help students understand the funnel illustration on Student Traitbook page 10. Topics may start out big, but as they go through the funnel, they become smaller and easier to manage.

Taming "Animals"

Ask students whether "animals" is too broad a topic, and have them explain their reasoning. If students do not recognize that "animals" is too general, try brainstorming a few of the things a writer could say about animals; students should quickly see how difficult it would be to handle this topic within a page or two. Go through the list of sample funnel questions together so that students can trace the way that questions help narrow this particular topic. Do they agree that the topic "Hunting Like a Snow Leopard" is narrow enough? If they do not, how would they narrow this topic further?

You Ask the Questions

In this part of the lesson, students work with partners. Explain that the pairs will be making up their own questions. *Who, What, When, Where, How, Which,* and *Is* are good ways to begin questions, but students should not feel restricted; they can ask any questions they like. The point is to help the writer focus on a narrow topic that is interesting to the writer and to readers. Remind students that three or four questions are usually enough to tame a topic. However, they can use more, if necessary.

At the end of this activity, students should review their topics to see whether they successfully narrowed them. Plan to share the topics aloud to see in how many different directions the students took the topic of "Fish." What does this variety tell you about large topics?

You Are the Tamer

Here, students will be working independently, but you should remind them that the process is essentially the same. The only real difference is that instead of having a partner to ask questions, they need to ask questions of themselves. In other words, they will ask the questions and come up with the answers. If students have any difficulty with this procedure (most should not), you can model it for them by beginning with a broad topic and asking yourself enough questions to narrow it down. Question yourself aloud so that students can follow your thinking process. Ask students to tell you when they think the topic is sufficiently narrow.

At the end of the exercise, partners should share their narrowed topics with each other. Then, you may wish to ask them to share with the class as a whole.

Extending the Lesson

- Make a list of "Before" and "After" topics. Present it as a class poster so that students can use it as a model for narrowing their writing topics.

- As you look at examples of strong, focused writing, try to imagine what broad topic the writer might have started with. Also decide, as a class, whether the writer's topic is narrow and focused enough.

- Ask each student to review a piece of writing on which he or she is currently working. With a partner, each student should read the writing aloud, determine what the main topic is, and decide whether it is sufficiently narrow. For topics that are still too broad, partners can help "funnel" them down to size.

Targeted Writing

For use with pages 12–15 in the Student Traitbook

In this lesson, students practice identifying the *main idea* in another writer's text. They also use a prewriting strategy to pinpoint their own main ideas. They then create original paragraphs in which the main idea is focused and easily identified.

Objectives

Students will learn that adding details does not create a main idea; it just creates a collection of details. Details must always connect to a central message: the bull's-eye of the target.

Skills Focus

- Understanding the concept of main idea
- Identifying the main idea in the writing of another—or recognizing the lack of a main idea
- Using the bull's-eye prewriting strategy to plan a piece of writing with a main idea and supporting details
- Writing a short paragraph based on the bull's-eye sketch

Time Frame

Allow about 40 minutes for this lesson. It can be broken into two parts. Part 1 would include analyzing and discussing Sample 1 and Sample 2 for the main idea, and then sketching out the bull's-eye (prewriting strategy) in preparation for a piece of personal writing (20 minutes). Part 2 would include using the bull's-eye sketch as a guide for generating a piece of original text (20 minutes).

Setting Up the Lesson

Before beginning the lesson, discuss with the class the concept of main idea. A main idea is a message that the writer wishes to convey: *Homemade pasta is easy and fun to make, wearing a helmet could save your life, scary movies do not give most people nightmares.*

A writer can choose one *topic* but not really have a main idea: *Cats make interesting pets. There are many kinds of cats. In the wild, cats will eat a wide variety of things. Of the large wild cats, cheetahs are the easiest to tame. I had a pet cat who lived to be 20.* This kind of writing has a topic—cats—but no main idea. Because this writing presents only a series of ideas, it has no clear central message.

On the overhead, create a piece of writing (like the one on "Cats") that sticks to one topic but has no main idea. Ask students to analyze the writing for a main idea. Does it have one? How do they know it does not? Look for answers like these:

- It skips around too much.

- It's hard to tell what the writer is trying to say.

- It never comes to the point.

- The different sentences do not relate to each other.

Now students should be ready to analyze and discuss Sample 1 and Sample 2.

Teaching the Lesson

Finding the Main Idea
Students may need to read Sample 1 and Sample 2 more than once.

Your Thoughts
Sample 1 is scattered and has no main idea. It jumps from the new addition, to the baby coming in October, to holiday birthdays, to self-esteem. The ideas are remotely connected, but this writer does not focus on a single point. Most students should see this writing as confusing and out of focus. Sample 2, on the other hand, is clearly focused. The main idea is stated in the first sentence: *It was so hot at my school the other day, I thought I would melt into my chair.* Other sentences relate directly to this main idea and build on the writer's message, helping readers understand exactly what it was like to be inside that school. Discuss the difference between the two pieces. Ask students to speculate about why one writer is so focused while the other is not.

The Bull's-eye

In the portion of the lesson on Student Traitbook page 14, students use a sketch of a target as a form of prewriting. The bull's-eye represents the main idea: the heart of the message. The surrounding circles provide space for the writer to add important details. Though the target can grow as large as a writer likes, the writing is more focused if the number of circles around the bull's-eye is held to a reasonable limit.

Strong Details for a Big Bull's-eye

Students should choose a topic about which they have a lot to say. Writers who find their topics interesting are less likely to wander.

Here students create their own bull's-eye sketches, using the model of the hot day at school as a guide. Remind them to ask themselves as they work whether the main idea is clear and focused. Does it make sense? Do all the details in the outer circles of the target relate to the main idea? If not, they can revise the main idea at any time or decide on a new one.

Your Target

Students should use their sketches to create their short paragraphs. As they work remind them to look carefully at their sketches in order to remember important details. They also should remain focused on the "bull's-eye," the main idea. Each detail sentence in the paragraph should connect clearly to this main sentence. If you ask students to share their writing, ask them to listen for the main idea and to be sure they can recognize this idea in one another's writing.

Extending the Lesson

- Share a piece of your own writing to see whether students can do a target sketch that shows your main idea as the bull's-eye and at least three or four supporting details.

- Ask students to give you a topic. Create a short paragraph that has no clear main idea. Then ask students to tell whether there is a main idea.

- Ask each student to review a piece of writing on which he or she is currently working. Can students do target sketches to represent main ideas and connecting details? If not, what can they do to make main ideas clearer?

Details on a Diet

For use with pages 16–19 in the Student Traitbook

In this lesson, students learn the importance of being selective with details so that readers feel satisfied but not overwhelmed.

Objectives

Students will understand that some details add no interest or instructional value to the writing. While it is important to tell readers enough to make the message clear, it is also important not to tell *everything* about a topic.

Skills Focus

- Identifying interesting information
- Writing a short paragraph that focuses on intriguing details

Time Frame

Allow about 30 minutes for this lesson.

Setting Up the Lesson

Choose any topic about which you think your students may have some knowledge, such as pets, things to see or do in your area, movies or TV shows worth watching, a particular sport or sporting event, a community event many people attend, or any topic at all. Then brainstorm a list of details related to the topic you chose. Write down every suggestion, whether or not it is interesting or relevant. When you have 15–20 details, stop. Then allow students to talk with partners and to select the five or six details they find most interesting or important. Talk about which details the class chose and why. Why are some details not worth including? How do you know?

> If I write what you know, I bore you; if I write what I know, I bore myself; therefore, I write what I don't know.
>
> —Robert Duncan

Teaching the Lesson

Sorting It Out: On or Off the Plate?

Students may need to read the list on Student Traitbook pages 17–18 more than once. They should read it quickly, asking questions such as "Is this interesting? Is this new information for me? Would I like to hear more?" This is a good time to introduce the concept of "common knowledge" for any students who might not be familiar with it. Explain that facts such as *Frogs live all over the world* or *Frogs can hop or jump* are known to most readers and will not add interest to the reading. Things known to most readers are called *common knowledge* and are usually best avoided in writing unless the audience has very little knowledge of the topic. What is common knowledge about frogs to a marine biologist would certainly not be common knowledge to a fifth-grade student.

Share and Compare

Give students time to compare the details they have selected. Did partners find many differences? Did they choose many of the same facts? Which were the most popular details throughout the class? Take some time to discuss the choices and the reasons for them.

Using Your "Plates" to Write

Encourage students to keep the number of details to about six. Before writing, each student may wish to look carefully at his or her short list of selected details to see whether a main idea stands out. Perhaps most of the details have to do with how frogs eat and drink, for instance. Remind students that selecting details is fun, but having a main idea that connects them is essential.

Extending the Lesson

- Ask students to share their frog paragraphs with the class. Discuss the different details students selected as being of interest, and also note which papers had a strong main idea.

- Ask students to try the same exercise again. This time, they should imagine that they are writing a chapter for a third-grade textbook. Would any of the details change? Why? Discuss how knowing the audience influences the details you choose.

- Invite each student to review a piece of writing from his or her writing folder. Suggest that students put a checkmark (or other indicator) next to each important or interesting detail. Then, have them underline each unnecessary detail. Give students time to revise according to the markings.

- Talk about ways to get information (films, reading, interviewing people, or visiting a site such as a museum or zoo) if students do not have enough important details in their writing.

Filling in the Details

For use with pages 20–23 in the Student Traitbook

A writer's own ideas are usually quite clear to him or her. Because the writer knows a topic well, he or she may not realize that details necessary for the reader's understanding or enjoyment are missing. Good writers learn to anticipate questions, amplify descriptions, and check to be sure that all the "holes" in the writing have been filled.

Objectives

Students will learn to identify the "holes" in their own or others' writing and understand the importance of relevant information.

Skills Focus

- Recognizing the need for additional details in writing
- Comparing strong, detailed writing to sketchy writing
- Identifying specific omissions in a sketchy piece of writing
- Posing questions that will help provide relevant details
- Creating an original piece of text that answers the questions raised

Time Frame

Allow about 35 minutes for this lesson.

Setting Up the Lesson

Some writing—"Swiss cheese" writing—is full of holes. In other words, important information has been left out. Keep in mind that your students have probably just completed a lesson (Lesson 3) that encouraged them to be selective in choosing details. Now we're telling them, "Don't leave out anything important!" This might sound like conflicting advice, but it is not. *Important* is the key word. Unneeded or obvious details should be left out. Holes in writing occur when a reader needs or wants information that the writer fails to provide.

Write a short sample piece in which you leave out some information. You might write about a scary or adventurous experience—anything with potential for excitement and interest. Don't tell much, though. Leave out important information. Then ask your students to help you fill in the holes by asking key questions.

Teaching the Lesson

Sharing an Example: *Harris and Me*

Read aloud Sample 1 on Student Traitbook page 21. Be sure to tell students that it is a revision of Gary Paulsen's original description of the character Louie. Ask for responses: Did students like it? Was anything left out? Are there any holes in this writing? Students should have many questions. Then read Sample 2 aloud as students read along with you. Ask them to compare the two samples. Students should not find many holes in this writing. Ask whether they can picture Louie. What is he like? What details stand out in their minds? There should be many.

Holes

Here students have a chance to write a list of questions to help them fill in missing information for a piece of writing. Students should read silently the piece called "Uncle Anthony" and then make a list of questions to help fill in the holes. Sample questions could include these:

- How tall is Uncle Anthony?

- Is his height the first thing you notice about him?

- Why does he always wear a hat?

- What special things does he do to make his visits so much fun?

- What does Uncle Anthony do that requires him to travel?

- Does he like to travel?

- What is your (the author's) favorite gift from Uncle Anthony? Why?

Filling in the Holes

Here's an opportunity for students to create some original writing based on the questions they have just listed. If they have done a good job of determining where the holes occur in "Uncle Anthony," revising the paragraph will be an easy task. If they have not, they will find it hard to write the paragraph. Students who have difficulty getting started may need to go back and list more questions or different questions. Also, ask students to reread the Gary Paulsen piece on Louie. Students should search for details that will make Uncle Anthony seem like a real person.

After students have revised the paragraph, ask them to compare their revisions with those of a partner. Which details were the same? Which details were different?

Extending the Lesson

- Ask students to check a passage from a math or science textbook. Have them list any missing information.

- Ask each student to write a short "Swiss cheese" paragraph in which he or she leaves plenty of holes. Then, have partners exchange papers and make lists of questions based on the missing information. Ask each student pair to select one of the samples and revise it, using their questions. Post the *before* and *after* samples for everyone to read.

- Have students check their current writing for missing information. Tell them to brainstorm questions to fix the problem. Students may revise as necessary.

Ideas

Teacher's Guide pages 5, 120–131
Overhead numbers 1–4

Objective

Students will review and apply what they have learned about the trait of ideas.

Reviewing Ideas

Review with students what they have learned about the trait of ideas. Ask students to discuss what ideas are and to explain why ideas are important in a piece of writing. Then ask them to recall the main points about ideas that are discussed in Unit 1. Students' responses should include the following points:

- Narrow the topic.
- Stay focused on the main topic.
- Choose the best details.
- Include all the information a reader needs.

Applying Ideas

To help students apply what they have learned about the trait of ideas, distribute copies of the Student Rubric for Ideas on page 5 of this Teacher's Guide. Students will use these to score one or more sample papers that can be found beginning on page 116. The papers for ideas are also on overheads 1–4.

Before students score the papers, explain that a rubric is a grading system to determine the score a piece of writing should receive for a particular trait. Preview the Student Rubric for Ideas, pointing out that a paper very strong in ideas receives a score of 6, and a paper very weak in ideas receives a score of 1. Tell students to read the rubric and then to read the paper to be scored. Then tell them to look at the paper and the rubric together to determine the score the paper should receive. Encourage students to make notes on each paper to help them score it. For example, they might put a check mark next to an interesting detail or draw a line through useless or irrelevant information.

Unit 2

Organization

Overview

In this unit, students study the concept of organization, the way a writer orders ideas. Organization is an internal structure much like the framework of a building. Once the building is up, you don't always see that structure, but it's still important in holding the building together. Similarly, once a piece of writing is complete, readers do not want to be overly conscious of the organization (e.g., *My next point will be . . .*). Still, it needs to be there, and it needs to be strong.

The focus of the instruction in this unit will be

- helping students recognize and write strong leads
- modeling the organization of details to make writing easy to follow and understand
- talking about the importance of staying with a main idea and not wandering from the topic
- helping students recognize and write strong conclusions

Organization: *A Definition*

Organization is about the logical and effective presentation of key ideas and details. Good organization keeps a piece of writing together and makes it easy to follow—like good instructions or a clear road map. The purpose for the writing strongly affects organization. For example, in a business letter, good organization might call for coming to the point quickly, getting through the main ideas efficiently, and bringing the letter to a quick conclusion.

The Unit at a Glance

The following lessons in the Teacher's Guide and practice exercises in the Student Traitbook will help develop understanding of the trait of organization. The Unit Summary provides an opportunity to practice evaluating papers for organization.

Unit Introduction: Organization

Teacher's Guide pages 20–24
Student Traitbook page 24

Students are introduced to the unique features of organization.

Lesson 5: Take Me to Your *Lead*-er

Teacher's Guide pages 25–27
Student Traitbook pages 25–28

Students will listen to a professional writer's lead, select a strong lead for each of two pieces of writing (one expository, one narrative), and create good leads of their own.

Lesson 6: That's an Order!

Teacher's Guide pages 28–30
Student Traitbook pages 29–32

Students reorganize a jumbled passage, working to put information into a logical and effective order.

Lesson 7: Sticking with It

Teacher's Guide pages 31–33
Student Traitbook pages 33–36

Students analyze a piece of writing for coherence. They also create an original piece in which all details are linked to a larger idea.

Lesson 8: Beware, the End Is Near!

Teacher's Guide pages 34–36
Student Traitbook pages 37–40

Students identify the hallmarks of a good conclusion, select the best conclusion for a piece from several possibilities, and craft conclusions of their own.

Unit Summary: Organization

Teacher's Guide page 37
Overhead numbers 5–8

Use the rubric on page 23 and the activities in the Summary to practice evaluating writing for organization.

Teacher Rubric for Organization

6
- The writer focuses on a single main point.
- The organizational pattern is suited to the topic, purpose, and audience.
- The lead engages the reader's attention and the conclusion is thoroughly satisfying.

5
- The writer seldom wanders from the main point.
- The organizational pattern fits the topic, purpose, and audience.
- The lead is appealing, and the conclusion works well.

4
- The writer may meander briefly, but not enough to distract or confuse the reader.
- The organizational pattern works most of the time.
- The lead and conclusion are fairly standard but functional.

3
- The writer wanders from the main point, confusing the reader.
- The organizational pattern is not well suited to this topic, purpose, or audience. It may be too formulaic or it may not follow a pattern.
- The lead and conclusion are present; one or both need work.

2
- Lack of order confuses the reader.
- The pattern is so formulaic that it's distracting—or there is no pattern.
- The lead and conclusion are missing or need work.

1
- The text is a disjointed collection of random thoughts.
- There is no identifiable structure or pattern.
- There is no real lead or conclusion.

Student Rubric for Organization

6
- My paper is easy to follow. It's like having a road map.
- I stick with one topic. I never wander.
- I chose an organizational pattern that fits my topic, purpose, and audience very well.
- My lead will grab the reader's attention.
- My conclusion sounds just right.

5
- My paper is easy to follow. The reader never feels lost.
- I stick with one topic—*almost* all the time.
- My organizational pattern fits my topic, purpose, and audience.
- My lead is very good. I worked on it.
- My conclusion is good, too.

4
- My paper is pretty easy to follow. I don't think the reader will get lost.
- I might have wandered a little from my main topic.
- I have an organizational pattern. I think it fits my purpose. I followed it most of the time.
- My lead works.
- My conclusion works, too.

3
- My paper is a little hard to follow. The reader will have to read *slowly*.
- I wandered from my main topic now and then.
- I tried to follow an organizational pattern. It might not go with my purpose.
- I have a lead, but I do not like it much.
- I have a conclusion, but I do not think it is very effective.

2
- My paper is hard to follow.
- I wrote about too many things. I forgot what my main idea was.
- I do not think there is a pattern here.
- I think I forgot to write a lead. The paper just starts.
- I don't have a strong conclusion. The paper just stops.

1
- This is just a bunch of ideas. No one could follow it.
- This doesn't make any sense. I don't even *have* a main topic yet.
- I don't have a pattern. Nothing goes with anything else.
- There is no lead or conclusion.

Recommended Books for Teaching Organization

Enhance lessons by sharing literature that relates to the trait of organization. Read the portion of a book that illustrates the writing feature you are teaching—strong leads or conclusions. As an alternative, read shorter passages in which the order is logical and easy to follow.

Caney, Steven. 1985. *Steven Caney's Invention Book*. New York: Workman Publishing. Here is nonfiction writing with many organizational patterns. This text also includes excellent leads and conclusions.

Fleischman, Paul. 1997. *Seedfolks*. New York: HarperCollins Publishers. This selection is a remarkable illustration of how to connect many smaller stories to one larger, organizing theme. It has powerful leads and conclusions.

———. 1999. *Weslandia*. Cambridge, MA: Candlewick Press. This has strong connections to a main idea, clear order, and an intriguing opening and conclusion.

Paulsen, Gary. 1998. *My Life in Dog Years*. New York: Delacorte Press. This features unusual organizational structure: a biography organized around the dogs Paulsen has owned. It includes strong leads and conclusions in each chapter.

Peck, Richard. 1998. *A Long Way from Chicago*. New York: Penguin Putnam. This selection offers a strong sense of order with a compelling lead and conclusion.

Sachar, Louis. 1998. *Holes*. New York: Farrar, Straus and Giroux. This is ideal for showing how a good lead sets up *everything* that follows.

Spandel, Vicki, with Ruth Nathan and Laura Robb. 2001. *The Daybook of Critical Reading and Writing* (Grade 5 edition). Wilmington, MA: Great Source. Excellent samples of leads, conclusions, support for main ideas, and organizational patterns in today's finest literature. Connects reading and writing.

More Ideas

Looking for more ideas on using literature to teach **organization?** We recommend *Books, Lessons, Ideas for Teaching the Six Traits: Writing in the Elementary and Middle Grades,* published by Great Source. Compiled and annotated by Vicki Spandel, this book is thoughtfully annotated and contains many lessons and ideas. For information, please phone 800-289-4490.

Take Me to Your Lead-er

For use with pages 24–28 in the Student Traitbook

In this lesson, students explore the importance of a strong lead as a way of getting and holding a reader's attention. By the end of the lesson, they should realize that drafting several possible leads for a piece of writing is well worth the effort, for without a strong lead, the writing may never be read.

Objectives

Students will practice identifying and writing strong leads.

Skills Focus

- Listening to a professional writer's lead to learn how to write effective leads
- Choosing the better of two leads
- Writing original leads and working with a partner to distinguish between strong and weak leads

Time Frame

Allow 40 minutes for this lesson. You can divide the lesson into two parts if you wish. Part 1 (20 minutes) includes listening to and discussing the opening lead and selecting the stronger lead for each of two pieces. Part 2 (20 minutes) includes writing original leads and sharing them with partners.

Setting Up the Lesson

Before beginning the lesson, introduce the concept of organization with Student Traitbook page 24. Then make sure every student knows that a lead is the way a writer sets the stage, hints at what is coming, and captures the reader's interest. Read leads from several books in your classroom. Ask students to identify the lead(s) they like best (as well as any they do not like) and to explain their preferences. Also talk about the strategies that the writers used to create effective leads.

> *I always begin with an image.*
> —Gabriel Garcia Marquez

Teaching the Lesson

Sharing an Example:
The Skin I'm In

Read aloud the first lead on Student Traitbook page 25, asking students to follow along. The lead is strong and suggests ominous things to come. It creates tension. Students should find themselves wondering who Miss Saunders is, who the writer is, and what is going to happen between them. You may wish to brainstorm a list of the students' questions or predictions.

Your Response

Encourage students to write their responses to this lead. They should tell whether they like it, what makes it work (or not work), any predictions they have, how it makes them feel, and so on. Share responses with the class.

Choosing the Lead-er

In this part of the lesson, students choose the stronger lead for each of two pieces of writing. The first piece is a story about a calf, and the other piece is an essay on snakes. From the possible leads for the calf story, most students should select Lead B. It has more voice and reveals the writer's fear for the young calf. It also offers much stronger images. Lead A is flat and tells only basic information. It does little to pique the reader's curiosity or raise questions about what will happen.

Of the possible leads for an essay on snakes, Lead A is the clear choice. It makes readers eager to learn more about snakes. In contrast, Lead B reports only that snakes are both scary and cool; the reader knows that, so there is little motivation for reading more. The lead isn't promising!

Share and Compare

Remember that some students may prefer the weaker lead. If this happens, encourage them to verbalize the reasons behind their choices, and invite other students to join the discussion.

Your Turn

Writing that is intentionally bad can be both amusing *and* instructive. Encourage your students to write weak leads. On the other hand, they should work hard with their good leads to create openings that will engage readers.

Share

Make sure that students read their leads aloud to each other and then share them with the whole class.

Extending the Lesson

- Ask each student to look at any piece of writing on which he or she is currently working. Ask students to write two new leads for their selections and then share them in a writing group. Which of the leads do their classmates like best?

- Ask each student to bring in a favorite book. Have each student share a lead and vote for a favorite. Then, make a list of ways to craft a lead.

- Try writing a lead and a conclusion—on separate pieces of paper—from three or four books. Mix them up and give them to students. Have students work in groups to see whether they can match the leads and conclusions that go together.

That's an Order!

For use with pages 29–32 in the Student Traitbook

This lesson is about putting information in logical order. During drafting, writers may write their ideas in almost any order. That strategy works when the point is to get all the information on paper without forgetting anything. During revision, however, it is important to look carefully and to read aloud, always asking whether the information presented comes in an order that is easy to follow—like a road map.

Objectives

Students will learn the importance of order in a piece of writing.

Skills Focus

- Listening for logical order in a piece of professional writing
- Comparing a disorganized piece to an ordered piece and discussing differences in readability
- Reordering a sample of disorganized writing

Time Frame

Allow 30 minutes for this lesson.

Setting Up the Lesson

Ask students whether they think that order is important. Here's a good way to illustrate this concept. Choose a recipe for something that students might enjoy—tacos, popcorn balls, or caramel apples, for example. Read the steps out of order. Be as disorganized as you can. You might end with a list of the ingredients (*"Oh, I forgot to tell you . . ."*) Then ask students whether they could follow the recipe and get satisfactory results.

Teaching the Lesson

Sharing an Example: *The Greedy Triangle*

Read both excerpts aloud, pausing after each one to ask students about the logical order of ideas. Students should find the first sample *very* disorganized. It is confusing, and events are difficult to follow. Without knowing the story, readers can make little sense of it.

Your Response

The second version, Burns's original, provides a sharp contrast to the first. The organization is logical, and most students should find the piece engaging and easy to understand. You might close by asking which version sounds most like the students' own writing. Be sure they write their responses.

Cleaning Up the Map

This is a challenging activity, and some students may need extra time. They must determine the correct order of eight sentences presented in random order: Have students read through the whole piece first, without deciding on the order. Then, have them read it again and mark their choices lightly in pencil so that they can change their minds. Next, have them read the paragraph aloud quietly to themselves to see whether they catch anything that is confusing or difficult to follow. Many hints within the paragraph should help students put the sentences in order.

Following is the correct order of the eight sentences. The first words are boldfaced to make them easier to find in the original:

It was supposed to be 90 degrees out, so we would need a great plan to keep ourselves from melting. **I thought we could start** the day with a water fight over at Cameron's house. **Cameron has a big front lawn,** perfect for water fights. **Around the middle of the day,** we could head to Carl's apartment for a swim. **The pool at Carl's house** has a small water slide in the deep end. **Later in the afternoon,** when it got really hot, we could hike into the woods to our fort. **There's so much shade** around the fort that it never gets too hot. **With a plan like this,** we were ready to beat the heat.

It may be possible to order some sentences somewhat differently and still have the paragraph make sense. Ultimately, the finished paragraph should be readable and easy to follow.

Share and Compare
This is the time for students to compare their work and to read paragraphs aloud again, listening for order. You want them to organize the information individually and then bring in a partner to help. When everyone has finished, discuss the "Great Cool-Off" paragraph as a class. What clues helped students put things in order?

Extending the Lesson

- Ask each student to read a piece of writing on which he or she is currently working to see whether the details or events are in order. Should anything be moved?

- Write a short paragraph (6–7 sentences). Be sure one or two of the sentences are clearly out of order. Ask students to tell you where your "map" got hard to follow and what can be done to fix it.

- Ask students to create a clear set of directions (at least 5 steps, no more than 8) for doing something simple, such as making a sandwich or selecting a good pair of shoes. They should write each step individually and skip a line or double-space between steps. Next, ask students to cut their directions into strips, mix them up, and exchange sets of strips with a partner. Finally, have each student put his or her set of steps into the right order.

- Have students brainstorm a list of things that writers can do to help make their writing easy to follow. Post the list in the classroom.

Lesson 7
Sticking with It

For use with pages 33–36 in the Student Traitbook

Sticking with one main idea is fine advice for writers, but it's easier said than done. Writers stand a better chance of making a message clear if they focus on one main idea and make sure that every detail connects to that idea.

Objectives

Students will learn to focus on a single main idea and realize the importance of anticipating readers' needs.

Skills Focus

- Identifying the main idea in a piece of writing
- Analyzing writing to determine whether it follows a main idea
- Thinking like a reader in reviewing one's own writing
- Revising a piece of writing to eliminate extraneous detail
- Creating an original piece of writing that focuses on a single, clearly stated main idea

Time Frame

Allow about 40 minutes for this lesson. You can divide the lesson into two parts: Part 1 (20 minutes) includes an analysis of "My Dad the Packer" and the prewriting activity (a brainstormed list). Part 2 (20 minutes) includes the creation of an original paragraph based on the brainstormed list.

Setting Up the Lesson

Ask each student to draw a rough map of the route from school to his or her home. Some students may find this easy, but many are likely to find it quite a challenge. When students have finished, ask them to discuss their maps. Then, talk about why it is so hard, even when you can picture something clearly in your mind, to make it just as clear on paper. What can students do if their maps are not as clear as they would like them to be? Should they retrace the route?

Explain that writing is a little like creating a map. Like map makers, writers can use specific strategies to make sure that ideas are clear and easy to follow. Writers need to brainstorm a list of important ideas, select a main idea, connect all details to the main idea, and organize their work in a logical order.

Teaching the Lesson

What's the BIG Idea?

This portion of the lesson allows students to decide whether another writer did a good job of creating a clear main idea and whether all the details connect to that main idea (they don't). Students will read "My Dad the Packer" individually and identify the main idea: *Dad has his own way of packing the car, and prefers to do all the work himself.* If students have difficulty with this, you can read the piece aloud.

Did the Author Stick or Stray?

This portion of the lesson asks students to revise, deleting any information that does not support the main topic. The following are irrelevant details and could be crossed out:

- Usually the garage is crowded with bikes, tools, and stuff from projects we are all working on, which makes it hard to find a place to put anything. There is always a clear path to the freezer where we keep the ice cream, frozen jam, and homemade applesauce. We always make applesauce after getting apples from the farm. It is great stuff!

- He has a pretty loud voice even when he talks on the phone. You should hear him cheer for our football team!

- He has a nice smile, and it shows up on every picture we have ever taken of him. When he was younger, he had braces, and now his teeth are nearly perfect. I'll probably have to have braces in another couple of years.

Students can cut almost half the copy without changing meaning. The cutting improves the piece by making it more concise, more organized, and easier to read.

Share and Compare

Make sure that students share with partners. Then discuss "My Dad the Packer" with the class. If students are timid about making cuts, share and explain the cuts you would make.

Your Turn

Students will complete a prewriting activity, listing things they recall about preparing for a family vacation or outing. **Tip:** At this point, they should not be too concerned about putting ideas in the right order. The point of the activity is to provide details about trip preparations. Later, they will decide what information to include. Then, they may wish to renumber details on the list so that the order makes sense. This makes the list much more useful in writing the paragraph.

Remind students that they can add details as they write their paragraphs. The list is an idea starter. It should *not* be restrictive in any way.

Extending the Lesson

- Brainstorm for ways writers can stay on topic when ideas are whirling faster than is possible to list. What can writers do to keep from wandering?

- Read aloud any well-written writing sample. Occasionally, insert a sentence that wanders from the topic. Ask students to identify the idea that does not fit.

- Ask each student to review a piece of his or her writing and to look specifically for any places that stray from the main topic. Have students delete this unnecessary information. They should then reread to make sure they have supplied enough information and that the main idea is easy to identify.

Beware, the End Is Near!

For use with pages 37–40 in the Student Traitbook

Good conclusions don't just stop and leave readers hanging, nor do they go on and on, trying to answer ALL the questions a reader could possibly have. They answer enough questions to make the writing feel finished. Like a good meal, a good conclusion satisfies but does not overwhelm.

Objectives

Students will differentiate between strong and weak conclusions and be able to write an original conclusion.

Skills Focus

- Identifying qualities of a strong conclusion through listening and discussion
- Choosing the strongest of three conclusions for a piece of writing
- Drafting a conclusion for an unfinished piece of writing

Time Frame

Allow 30–40 minutes for this lesson. Some students may need more time because of the extended reading and the writing activity at the end. The lesson can be divided into two parts. In Part 1 (20 minutes) students will listen to and discuss the conclusion to *The Wreckers* and then select the best conclusion for "Lost in the Storm." In Part 2 (20 minutes), students will read and draft a conclusion for "Pieces of Eight."

Setting Up the Lesson

Discuss the importance of a good conclusion. Read several examples of conclusions with the class. (See the list of recommended books on page 24 of this Teacher's Guide.) Ask students to state specifically what they like or do not like about each conclusion. Brainstorm a list of the characteristics of good conclusions. Ask students to explain how a good conclusion should sound and what it should accomplish.

Teaching the Lesson

Sharing an Example:
The Wreckers

This passage on Student Traitbook page 37 has a strong conclusion. Ask students to explain why this ending is effective. Would it ruin the story if the narrator went on? (For example, *Of course, most people don't believe in the corpse lights now and you can't see them on a moonlit night anyhow, especially with all the tourists on the beach. . . .*) Point out that any time *going on* spoils the mood or erases a wonderful lingering image in your mind, you can be sure that the story is over.

Your Response

Take time to share students' written reactions, and talk about how the conclusion made them feel. Feelings can be as important to good writing as thoughts.

Select a Conclusion

Have students read "Lost in the Storm," on Student Traitbook page 39, on their own. If any students struggle with it, you can read aloud as they follow along. Make sure students understand the essentials of the story, so that they will be able to determine what kind of ending works best. Ask whether this is a happy story. Is it funny? Is it scary? What is the writer worried about? What *could* happen? Do you think this writer will solve his problem?

What's Your Choice?

Most students will choose Conclusion 3. This strong conclusion depicts the writer's true state of mind: He is hardly aware of his own discomfort (*I couldn't think . . . I forced myself . . . I don't really remember . . .*), and can focus only on saving Meeka. In this version, Meeka has a personality, too; she is frightened and has run away. These details strengthen the appeal of the story and its realistic conclusion. Meeka is a real dog.

Point out to students that Conclusion 2 provides only facts. It is an example of how to wrap things up as quickly as possible. In your discussion of Conclusion 2, remind students *never* to put the words "The End" on any piece of writing. To do so is always unnecessary.

Conclusion 1 has possibilities. The writer is courageous, running into the storm and ignoring the cries of his frightened parents. In this version, Meeka is lively enough to bark and leap into the owner's arms, but it's still less dynamic than Conclusion 3.

Your Hallway, Your EXIT, Your Turn

Before they write, ask students to recall some of the conclusions you have shared. Ask, "What should a good conclusion do?" or "How should a good conclusion sound?" Then ask them to write a conclusion to "Pieces of Eight." Encourage students to write more than one conclusion if they have time and then to choose the favorite. Ask them to imagine that they will be writing a conclusion to a short story in a magazine. If the conclusion is good, the magazine may publish another story. **Tips and Questions:** Think of Ann as a real person. Imagine how she feels. Imagine what *could* be in the box. Will Ann be surprised when she finds out? Will the readers? Remember that a good conclusion answers some questions but not necessarily ALL.

Share and Compare

Allow a few minutes for student partners to share their completed passages. How are the new endings alike or different?

Extending the Lesson

- Share your own conclusion for "Pieces of Eight." Talk about the ways your conclusion differed from those written by your students.

- As you're reading aloud a story, chapter, or essay, stop just before the conclusion to ask students to predict how the piece will end. Write out these predictions so that students can refer to them as you read the conclusion. Ask, "What is the connection between predictions and conclusions?"

- Ask students to write an alternate conclusion for "Lost in the Storm." Suggest that they try writing the conclusion from the point of view of the mom or the dog. You may wish to give students at-home time for this. Be sure to read results aloud.

- Make a collection of favorite conclusions from literature you have read in class or from other sources. Make a poster displaying the results.

Organization

Teacher's Guide pages 23, 132–143
Overhead numbers 5–8

Objective

Students will review and apply what they have learned about the trait of organization.

Reviewing Organization

Review with students what they have learned about the trait of organization. Ask students to discuss what organization means and to explain why it is important in a piece of writing. Then ask them to recall the main points about organization that are discussed in Unit 2. Students' responses should include the following points:

- Write a strong lead.
- Put information in an order that makes sense.
- Stay on topic.
- Write a strong conclusion.

Applying Organization

To help students apply what they have learned about the trait of organization, distribute copies of the Student Rubric for Organization on page 23 of this Teacher's Guide. Students will use these to score one or more sample papers that can be found beginning on page 116. The papers for organization are also on overheads 5–8.

Before students score the papers, explain that a rubric is a grading system to determine the score a piece of writing should receive for a particular trait. Preview the Student Rubric for Organization, pointing out that a paper that is well organized receives a score of 6, and a paper that is not organized receives a score of 1. Tell students to read the rubric and then to read the paper to be scored. Then tell them to look at the paper and the rubric together to determine the score the paper should receive. Encourage students to make notes on each paper to help them score it. For example, they might put a check mark next to a strong lead or conclusion and an X next to a weak lead or conclusion.

Unit 3
Voice

Overview

In this unit, students explore the concept of voice, the way in which a writer lets his or her personality and perspective show through the writing. Voice is part individuality, part energy and emotion, and part audience connection. Students should see voice as a powerful means of enhancing ideas.

The focus of the instruction in this unit will be
- showing students how to match voice with purpose
- modeling ways to revise writing that is weak in voice
- encouraging students to imitate voices they admire as a way of "trying on" another writer's voice
- coaching students to write with a strong voice

Voice: *A Definition*

Because voice is such a hallmark of individuality, it has sometimes been called "the fingerprints of the writer on the page." As one teacher put it, your ideas are what you have to say; the voice is how you say it. Voice is personality, concern for the needs of an audience, energy and enthusiasm, and that quality that keeps readers reading. Voice is distinctive and tends to become more so as the writer practices his or her craft and becomes increasingly aware of personal voice. Voice also changes with purpose. The voice of a letter to the editor is different from the voice in a newspaper headline story—or the voice in mystery or poem.

The Unit at a Glance

The following lessons in the Teacher's Guide and practice exercises in the Student Traitbook will help develop understanding of the trait of voice. The Unit Summary provides an opportunity to practice evaluating papers for voice.

Unit Introduction: Voice

Teacher's Guide pages 38–42
Student Traitbook page 41

Students are introduced to the trait of voice.

Lesson 9: Matching Voice and Purpose

Teacher's Guide pages 43–45
Student Traitbook pages 42–45

Students will see that different voices are suited to different writing tasks. Students will describe voices, identify the writer's purpose from voice used, and analyze the suitability of voice to purpose.

Lesson 10: Raising Your Voice

Teacher's Guide pages 46–48
Student Traitbook pages 46–49

Students rank three samples based on voice and then strengthen one of the weaker samples by adding detail or altering the wording.

Lesson 11: All-Star Voices

Teacher's Guide pages 49–51
Student Traitbook pages 50–53

Students listen to a strong passage, discuss it, and then share favorite passages of their own in small groups. They practice oral reading and listening skills, discuss differences across a range of voices, and select a favorite voice to imitate.

Lesson 12: It's All About You

Teacher's Guide pages 52–54
Student Traitbook pages 54–57

Students will think about the importance of individuality—using a personal perspective to create a powerful, unique voice. They bring strategies learned in previous lessons together to select a topic and create original writing with strong voice.

Unit Summary: Voice

Teacher's Guide page 55
Overhead numbers 9–12

Use the rubric on page 41 and the activities in the Summary to practice evaluating writing for strong and appropriate voice.

Teacher Rubric for Voice

6
- This voice is as individual as a fingerprint.
- The reader will want to read this aloud to someone.
- The writing is passionate and compelling.
- The voice is perfect for the purpose and audience.

5
- This voice is individual—probably recognizable if the reader knows the writer.
- The reader would probably share this piece aloud.
- The writing shows strong feelings and is appealing to read. It has a lot of energy.
- The voice is suitable for the audience and purpose.

4
- This voice is distinctive, if not unique.
- The reader might share *moments* of this piece aloud.
- Passion, energy, or strong feelings are evident in some places.
- The voice is acceptable for the audience and purpose, but it could use refining.

3
- This is a functional, sincere voice, though not especially distinctive.
- The piece does not seem ready to share aloud.
- Moments of passion, energy, or strong feelings are rare. The reader needs to look.
- The voice may not seem quite right for the purpose or audience.

2
- The voice is not at all distinctive. It does not stand out.
- The piece is definitely not ready to share aloud.
- This writing could use a serious energy boost. The writer sounds bored.
- The voice does not seem appropriate for the purpose or audience.

1
- This voice is difficult to find, identify, or describe.
- Lack of voice means that the reader probably will not share this by reading aloud.
- No energy or excitement comes through.
- The voice is missing or inappropriate for the audience and purpose.

Student Rubric for Voice

6
- This is me. The reader can tell that this is my voice.
- I think the reader will *definitely* want to share this paper aloud with someone.
- I love my topic, and my enthusiasm and energy come through.
- The voice of this piece is perfect for my purpose and audience.

5
- This voice sounds mostly like me.
- The reader might want to share this paper aloud.
- I like this topic, so a lot of energy comes through.
- The voice is just right for my purpose and audience.

4
- This paper sounds like me in parts.
- A reader might share some moments here and there.
- I like this topic pretty well. The writing has *some* energy.
- My voice seems right for my purpose and audience.

3
- I am not sure whether this paper sounds like me.
- I don't think this is quite ready to share aloud.
- The topic is all right, but I could not get too excited about it.
- I do not know whether this voice fits my purpose and audience.

2
- I do not think this sounds much like me.
- This is not ready to share aloud.
- I did not like this topic. I could not get excited about it.
- I don't have much voice, and I am not sure what my purpose is or who my audience might be.

1
- I do not hear *any* voice in this writing.
- I would not share this aloud.
- I did not like this topic one bit. It was boring.
- I do not know my purpose or my audience for this.

Recommended Books for Teaching Voice

Share samples of literature rich in voice. Choose books you enjoy reading aloud, and remember that you can share a whole book, a chapter, or just a passage. Read with expression. Always ask students, *Do you hear the voice? Did this piece have more voice than the previous one? What voices that we have shared this week spoke to you most?* Students' own writing voices are different, as are their preferences, so do not be surprised if some students prefer some voices to others. Readers are often drawn to voices that echo some portion of their own personalities.

Branzei, Sylvia. 1997. *Grossology Begins at Home: the Science of Really Gross Things in Your Everyday Life.* New York: Addison Wesley Longman. This selection includes intriguing details presented with lots of voice—nonfiction content.

Ehrlich, Amy, ed. 1996. *When I Was Your Age.* Cambridge, MA: Candlewick Press. These memoirs contain great expression and detail.

Little, Jean. 1986. *Hey, World, Here I Am!* New York: HarperCollins Publishers. This coming-of-age tale reveals multiple voices: wistful, reflective, angry, humorous.

Littlechild, George. 1993. *This Land Is My Land.* San Francisco: Children's Book Press. Here is a serious, respectful voice, focusing on heritage.

Paulsen, Gary. 1998. *Soldier's Heart.* New York: Bantam Doubleday Dell Publishing. This selection combines fact and fiction in an honest, revealing voice about a young soldier's realization of what war is.

Scieszka, Jon. 1995. *Math Curse.* New York: Viking. This story includes an honest, tongue-in-cheek voice about struggling with math.

Spandel, Vicki, with Ruth Nathan and Laura Robb. 2001. *The Daybook of Critical Reading and Writing* (Grade 5 edition). Wilmington, MA: Great Source. This provides excellent samples of voice, fictional and nonfictional, serious to hilarious, in today's finest literature. Connects reading and writing.

More Ideas

Looking for more ideas on using literature to teach voice? We recommend *Books, Lessons, Ideas for Teaching the Six Traits: Writing in the Elementary and Middle Grades,* published by Great Source. Compiled and annotated by Vicki Spandel. This book is thoughtfully annotated and contains many lesson ideas. For information, please phone 800-289-4490.

Matching Voice and Purpose

For use with pages 41–45 in the Student Traitbook

This lesson is about matching the voice in writing to the purpose. Students need to hear a variety of voices, and then determine how each voice supports a writer's purpose, such as a reflective voice for poetry, a dark and ominous voice for mystery, a comic or natural voice for personal narrative or essay, a formal voice for business correspondence, and so on.

Objectives

Students will connect the writer's voice to the writer's purpose.

Skills Focus

- Identifying the kind of voice a writer uses
- Finding words to describe various voices
- Inferring the writer's purpose from the voice of a piece
- Determining whether a particular voice is suited to the writer's purpose

Time Frame

Allow 30–35 minutes for this lesson.

Setting Up the Lesson

Ask students to think about the voices they use in real life, and help them make a list. Then ask them to think about when they use these different voices. Explain that voice reflects purpose, and that one voice cannot suit every purpose. This is as true for writing as it is for speaking. Use the unit introduction on Student Traitbook page 41 to reinforce the concept of voice.

Teaching the Lesson

Sharing an Example:
Soldier's Heart

Before sharing this sample aloud (Student Traitbook pages 42–43), remind students to listen for voice. Have them determine the *kind* of voice being used and try to describe it. Words that describe voice are provided at the end of the selection, but students can add to this list if they wish. Of the words provided, those that come closest to describing the voice are probably *serious, tense,* and *quiet.* Charley is *excited* about joining the Army but *worried* about being accepted. The narrator uses a *quiet* but *forceful* voice.

The Reason for Writing: Using Voice As a Clue

This part of the lesson is meant to help students understand that writers write for different purposes, and voice provides a clue to an author's purpose. For example, if the voice is humorous, the writer might wish to entertain readers and make them laugh. If the voice is serious or formal, the writer may wish to persuade or inform readers.

Students are invited to read on their own the Stephen Kramer piece from *Caves.* Remind them to ask themselves as they read, "What kind of voice is this? Why would a writer choose this voice?" Words to describe the voice in Sample 2 might include *serious, reflective, instructional, thoughtful,* or *quiet.* The writer uses this voice to teach readers about caves.

On-Key or Off-Key Voice?

Off-key singing is irritating. Writing in which the voice does not match the purpose can be similarly annoying. In the business letter on Student Traitbook page 44, the voice is wrong for a business letter—though the writer is certainly friendly and projects a lot of voice. The voice in the letter should be more restrained and businesslike. The voice in this letter is chatty and excited (the pitch is almost hysterical). This voice could work in a letter to a friend or in a personal story, but it is not appropriate in a business letter.

Extending the Lesson

- Give students a list of writing situations, and see whether they can come up with a voice suited to each one:

    1. a newspaper article about electricity blackouts resulting from a power shortage

    2. a thank-you letter to grandparents for a great birthday gift

    3. an article explaining how to swim

    4. a story about a time the writer was really embarrassed

- Continue to read aloud from favorite pieces with strong voice. Share pieces that are weak in voice: textbook excerpts, encyclopedias, brochures, contracts, some business letters, and samples from junk mail. In each case, ask students to identify the kind of voice they hear and to say whether it matches the purpose for writing.

- Invite students to read aloud from favorite pieces in which the voice is strong. They might also wish to share pieces that seem to lack voice.

Raising Your Voice

For use with pages 46–49 in the Student Traitbook

In this lesson, students use their analytical skills to rank three narrative voices and decide which is strongest. In doing this, they will be readers *and* listeners. If they can hear the voice in their heads as they read, they will have an easier time with the assessment. As part of the assessment, students will revise a writing sample they found to be weak in voice.

Objectives

Students will sharpen skills in identifying strong voice and practice revising a weaker piece to make it strong in voice.

Skills Focus

- Listening for voice
- Ranking three passages according to the strength of the voice in each
- Revising a weaker piece to make the voice stronger

Time Frame

Allow 35 minutes for this lesson, excluding Extending the Lesson. Some students may need slightly longer to finish the revision portion of the lesson. If so, you can extend the lesson into the following day.

Setting Up the Lesson

Two skills are critical in this lesson: determining the strength of voice from a series of examples and revising a piece that is weak in voice. Prepare students for the first part by discussing the elements they should listen for when they listen for voice. Share with students the Student Rubric for Voice on page 41 in this Teacher's Guide. Encourage them to listen for the elements described in the rubric as you read aloud during the lesson. Remind the students to refer to their rubrics as often as necessary.

The best way to prepare students for the revision portion of the lesson is by modeling. Write a short paragraph with little or no voice. Ask students for suggestions on how you can improve the voice.

Teaching the Lesson

Rank the Voice

Read aloud the three pieces on pages 47–48 in the Student Traitbook, and encourage students to make notes as you read. For example, they might wish to underline examples of strong voice. "The Climbing Wall" has rich, powerful, sustained voice; this writer really sets the scene and puts himself or herself into the writing. "Fireworks" has a somewhat weaker voice. It's a series of statements with little elaboration or authority. "Picking Blackberries" has moments of voice (for example, *We act like spies on a top-secret mission. . . .*), but the voice fades in and out like poor radio reception.

Talk About the Voices

Be sure students rank the three pieces. Discuss these rankings before moving on to the next lesson, and ask students to give specific reasons for their decisions.

From a Whisper to a Shout!

This portion of the lesson on Student Traitbook page 48 calls for students to revise a piece weak in voice. Students should choose "Fireworks" or "Picking Blackberries." You may wish to list some ways of making voice stronger, such as showing feelings and enthusiasm, using words that reveal emotions, including specific details that put the reader right at the scene, and so on. Post this list so that students can refer to it as they work.

Share and Compare

Invite volunteers to share revisions, and applaud any improvements in voice, however slight. Some students may not go all the way to a shout, but even a moment of added voice is an improvement. As a class, you may wish to identify the moments you liked best.

Extending the Lesson

- Invite students to write a passage weak in voice, and then write a "revised" version, putting in plenty of voice. They can read "before" and "after" examples in their response groups, identifying elements various writers use to add voice.

- Read aloud from any passage you think is strong in voice. See whether students can identify what makes the passage strong in voice.

- Have students make a list of "Tips for Strong Voice." Post the list where students can refer to it easily.

- Invite each student to review a piece of his or her writing and decide whether the voice is a whisper or a shout. Students who have achieved only a whisper should ask what they can do to revise for stronger voice.

All-star Voices

For use with pages 50–53 in the Student Traitbook

This lesson invites students to listen to different voices. Each student will also imitate a favorite voice. The strategy of imitating a different voice helps the student develop an individual voice.

Objectives

Students will discover new voices and improve individual voice by imitating that of another writer.

Skills Focus

- Listening for voice
- Identifying favorite voices
- Reading aloud with expression to share voices
- Imitating another writer's voice as one strategy for building voice

Time Frame

Allow time for students to select a favorite book to share. On Day 1 (15 minutes), share the Konigsburg example and begin talking about favorite voices—your favorites included. Then, on Day 2, give students time to share in groups (15 minutes) and time to try imitating one favorite voice (15–20 minutes).

Setting Up the Lesson

Share moments of voice from some of your favorite authors. Read with expression, and remind students to do so in their writing groups when they share their favorites. Be sure to explain why you chose each piece, pointing out what makes each voice special. As you share the reasons for your selections, you increase students' understanding of what voice is all about.

> *Every book should have its own voice—what you hear in your head as you read to yourself.*
>
> —Mary Lee Settle

Teaching the Lesson

Sharing an Example: *Silent to the Bone*

Read the passage aloud, or have students read silently. Ask students to describe the voice and what the voice tells the reader about Connor.

Listen and Learn

Ask students to share their responses. What kind of voice did they hear?

An All-Star Voice

Tell students that they will have time to select their favorite passages. Encourage students to visit the library, and remind them to explore books at home. A personal library in the classroom is a good place for students to look, too. Some students may wish to share a passage from a magazine or newspaper article. This is acceptable as long as the passage presents an example of voice that they think they can imitate. Encourage students to look for examples of a strong voice that really stands out.

When students have selected their passages, organize them in small response groups. Each student will read his or her passage aloud in the group. Be sure students rehearse briefly before sharing favorite passages. They should read aloud to themselves—more than once if necessary—so that they feel confident enough to bring out the voice.

Trying Another Voice

Imitating another writer's voice is not easy, but the process is valuable. Expect students to feel challenged, and provide extra time for those who need it. Encourage students to discuss the voice they wish to imitate with others in their group before writing and to find words that describe it: *irritated, shy, thoughtful, funny, timid, frightened, nervous, outgoing, silly, friendly, excited,* and so on.

Imitation gets easier through practice, so you may wish to return to this lesson several times through the year, each time asking students to choose a different voice to imitate or a different passage illustrating the same voice.

Extending the Lesson

- Talk about what happens when you try to imitate someone else's voice. Do you lose a little of your own voice, or does the other person's voice enhance your own? Is either result a good thing?
- Make a list of favorite voices that your students have discovered through the course of this lesson. Turn this into a poster, and keep it on the wall as a reminder.
- See whether students can define the term *voice.* Make a poster of their definitions.

It's All About You

For use with pages 54–57 in the Student Traitbook

This lesson celebrates the individual. Encourage your students to consider what makes them individuals, and remind them that voice is the expression of the writer as an individual.

Objectives

Students will enhance their personal writing as they let their voices "out of the bag" by writing a personal, original piece of writing.

Skills Focus

- Thinking about personally important topics
- Choosing a personally important topic about which to write
- Prewriting
- Creating a piece of writing with strong voice
- Using descriptive words to explain one's personal voice
- Assessing a piece of personal writing for voice

Time Frame

Allow at least 35 minutes for this lesson, excluding Extending the Lesson. Some students may require more time to complete the writing activity, so extend the lesson into a second day if necessary. If you want students to share and revise what they have written, add another 30 minutes.

Setting Up the Lesson

Because this is a lesson about individuality, why not start with yourself? Write and share a short list of details that describe who you are. Start with the line "What makes me ME . . ." and add details that define a unique individual. Invite each student to make a similar list.

List some topics you or your students might like to write about. Brainstorm as many topics as possible. Many ideas can come from those personal "What makes me ME" lists. Remind students that it is important for them to choose topics about which they have strong feelings, thoughts, or opinions. Point out that to develop a distinct and believable voice, the writer must care about the topic.

Teaching the Lesson

Setting the Channel to MSV

Now students will choose their topics. They should have two lists: the one in the Student Traitbook and the one you brainstormed together. They may also suggest new topics at this time. Tell students to ask themselves these questions: "Will I enjoy writing about this topic? Can I put voice into a paper about this topic?" If the answer to either or both questions is no, the students should consider other topics.

A Little Push

Are your students accustomed to prewriting or brand new to it? Their experience will affect the amount of time you spend on this activity. If students are not familiar with how to make an idea web, create a word collection, or list questions, model these for them. Consider modeling at least two prewriting strategies that *you* know and use. Then encourage students to take time for this important part of writing. Prewriting starts the thought process and usually leads to much stronger voice.

Write! Write! Write!

When students have finished prewriting, give them time to begin their drafts. They should have at least 15 minutes of uninterrupted writing time. Stretch it to 20 minutes if their attention spans will allow. During this time, you can circulate, answering questions and offering suggestions to students who are having difficulties. When students cannot think of what to write, have them ask these questions: (1) Can the reader *picture* it? (The writer must put an image in the reader's mind) and (2) Can the reader *feel* it? Remind students to let feelings come through in their writing. Writing with voice lets the reader participate fully in the writer's experience. It lets the reader see and feel as the writer sees and feels.

Rest and Reflect

This part of the lesson allows for some personal reflection, and you may want to guide students through the process. Each student is asked to describe his or her own voice. This is challenging, so you may wish to list some possibilities, such as *funny, angry, sad, lazy, frantic, worried, joyful, excited,* and so on.

You Be the Judge

Students are asked to rate themselves on the trait of voice. Remind them to be honest. If the voice is weak or absent, they should record that fact and think of ways to make the voice stronger. However, if the voice *is* powerful, make sure they give themselves high scores. You may also wish to allow time for students to share their writing and to extend their revisions based upon that sharing.

Extending the Lesson

- Rate other pieces of writing for voice, and discuss what gives the stronger pieces their power—as well as what is lacking from the pieces with weaker voice.

- Write letters, individually or as a class. You can write to local business people, asking for information or commenting on something students appreciate in your community, or to sports figures, celebrities, musicians, or favorite authors. Read some of the letters aloud, and make a class book with letters and responses. Which responses have the most voice? Why?

- Encourage students to rate their own writing for voice and to try to strengthen the voice of each piece.

- Model ways to improve voice by writing some pieces weak in voice and inviting students to make the voice stronger. Then have students rate the voice of the "before" and "after" pieces. Did the voice improve?

Voice

Teacher's Guide pages 41, 144–155
Overhead numbers 9–12

Objective

Students will review and apply what they have learned about the trait of voice.

Reviewing Voice

Review with students what they have learned about the trait of voice. Ask students to discuss what voice means and to explain why it is important in a piece of writing. Then ask them to recall the main points about voice that are discussed in Unit 3. Students' responses should include the following points:

- Match voice with purpose.
- Revise to make voice stronger.
- Imitate a favorite voice.
- Write with a strong voice.

Applying Voice

To help students apply what they have learned about the trait of voice, distribute copies of the Student Rubric for Voice on page 41 of this Teacher's Guide. Students will use these to score one or more sample papers that can be found beginning on page 116. The papers for voice are also on overheads 9–12.

Before students score the papers, explain that a rubric is a grading system to determine the score a piece of writing should receive for a particular trait. Preview the Student Rubric for Voice, pointing out that a paper very strong in voice receives a score of 6, and a paper very weak in voice receives a score of 1. Tell students to read the rubric and then to read the paper to be scored. Then tell them to look at the paper and the rubric together to determine the score the paper should receive. Encourage students to make notes on each paper to help them score it. For example, they might put a check mark next to sentences in which a strong voice emerges.

Word Choice
Unit 4

Overview

This unit emphasizes word choice. Students will learn that good writers make choices based on specific strategies: using verbs to energize writing, eliminating clutter, and using sensory words to create vivid pictures and impressions.

The focus of the instruction in this unit will be

- increasing students' awareness of the power of strong verbs
- giving students practice in extracting word meaning from context
- encouraging students to enrich their writing with sensory detail that helps readers take part in the writer's experience
- showing students how to cut "clutter" from inflated writing

Word Choice: *A Definition*

Word Choice refers to the language a writer chooses to express his or her ideas. Good word choice is clear, colorful, and precise. The more precise the word choice, the clearer the meaning. *Tree* is not as precise, for instance, as *birch* or *Dutch elm*. Strong word choice lets the reader see, hear, smell, touch, and taste the world of the writer. Secrets to successful word choice include the use of powerful verbs and of sensory detail, and the variety that comes from an expanded vocabulary. As with any trait, appropriate word choice depends on audience and purpose. In a business letter, writing should be crisp, clear, and to the point. In creative writing, the writer is free to be playful with language.

The Unit at a Glance

The following lessons in the Teacher's Guide and practice exercises in the Student Traitbook will help develop understanding of the trait of word choice. The Unit Summary provides an opportunity to practice evaluating papers for word choice.

Unit Introduction: Word Choice

Teacher's Guide pages 56–60
Student Traitbook page 58

Students are introduced to the unique features of word choice.

Lesson 13: Lights, Camera, Action!

Teacher's Guide pages 61–63
Student Traitbook pages 59–62

Students will take control of their writing by choosing verbs that enliven the writing and help the reader feel and picture the action.

Lesson 14: Headline News—Use Writer's Clues!

Teacher's Guide pages 64–66
Student Traitbook pages 63–66

Students learn the meaning of *context* and use context clues to make educated guesses about the meaning of new words.

Lesson 15: Painting Word Pictures

Teacher's Guide pages 67–69
Student Traitbook pages 67–70

Students listen for effective, striking sensory language and try their hands at becoming "word artists."

Lesson 16: Brush Strokes, Not Buckets!

Teacher's Guide pages 70–72
Student Traitbook pages 71–74

Students learn to make each word count and rid their writing of clutter.

Unit Summary: Word Choice

Teacher's Guide page 73
Overhead numbers 13–16

Use the rubric on page 59 and the activities in the Summary to practice evaluating writing for word choice.

Teacher Rubric for Word Choice

6
- The writing is clear, striking, original, and precise.
- The writer uses powerful verbs to enliven the writing.
- Sensory language, as appropriate, enhances meaning.
- The writing is concise; each word counts.

5
- The writing is clear and often original.
- The writer relies more on strong verbs than on modifiers to enrich meaning.
- Sensory language, as appropriate, adds detail.
- The writing is reasonably concise; a word or phrase here and there could be cut.

4
- The writing is clear in most cases. Some words or phrases are vague or confusing.
- The writer uses some strong verbs and may rely too heavily on modifiers.
- Sensory language is present, if needed.
- Some writing is concise; wordy moments are noticeable.

3
- The writing is often unclear, misleading, or vague, though the main idea comes through.
- The reader needs to hunt for strong verbs. Modifiers may be overused.
- Sensory language is minimal or else overused.
- The writing may be short, but, it is not necessarily concise. Some clutter is evident.

2
- Many words and phrases are misused, vague, or unclear. The writer's main message is not clear.
- Strong verbs are rare or missing.
- Sensory language is minimal or absent.
- Word use may be skimpy *or* cluttered; either way, meaning is hard to determine.

1
- Words and phrases are vague, confusing, or misused.
- Verbs are weak throughout; this writing is flat and boring.
- Sensory language is missing.
- Word choice is imprecise and inhibits clarity.

Student Rubric for Word Choice

6
- Every word helps make my meaning clear.
- My verbs are powerful and lively—they energize my writing.
- My words paint a clear picture in the reader's mind.
- I eliminated any clutter.

5
- My words are clear most of the time.
- I used a lot of strong verbs.
- My words paint a picture. The reader can tell what I'm trying to say.
- I got rid of clutter. I don't think it's a problem.

4
- My words are clear most of the time. The reader can identify my main idea.
- I used some strong verbs. I guess I could use more.
- Some of my words paint a picture. Some are vague.
- My writing has *some* clutter.

3
- My words are often unclear. The reader needs to guess my main idea.
- I think I have *some* strong verbs. I need to look, though.
- The reader might be able to picture what I am talking about if he or she works at it.
- My writing is cluttered. I used too many unnecessary words.

2
- My words are *very* unclear. It is hard to tell what I am saying.
- I do not know whether I used any verbs. I am not sure what a verb is.
- It is hard to picture what I am talking about.
- I do not know whether I used too many words or not enough words. I just wrote.

1
- My words are hard to understand. I am not sure what I want to say.
- I do not know whether I used verbs. What is a verb?
- I don't think the reader can picture what I am talking about.
- Maybe I used too many words. Maybe I used the wrong words. I don't know.

Recommended Books for Teaching Word Choice

As you share literature—strong or weak in word choice—remember to ask your students questions like these: *Which words did you like? Did you hear any new words you could add to your personal dictionary? Did you hear any vague or overused words? Did you notice any verbs or sensory words that added power or detail to the writing?*

DiCamillo, Kate. 2001. *The Tiger Rising.* Cambridge, MA: Candlewick Press. This selection contains straightforward, concise language and strong verbs. The language is never overdone.

Henkes, Kevin. 1997. *Sun & Spoon.* New York: Puffin Books. This selection exemplifies simple language used well—excellent for modeling.

Holt, Kimberly Willis. 1999. *When Zachary Beaver Came to Town.* New York: Henry Holt and Company. This story uses concise language to tell an unforgettable story.

Kemper, Dave, with Ruth Nathan, Patrick Sebranek, and Carol Elsholz. 2000. *Writers Express: A Handbook for Young Writers, Thinkers, and Learners.* Wilmington, MA: Great Source. This book reveals all the writers' secrets you need to bring the trait of word choice to life.

Nye, Bill. 1993. *Bill Nye the Science Guy's Big Blast of Science.* Mercer Island, WA: Tvbooks, Inc. This selection provides refreshingly lively language used in informational writing.

Peck, Richard. 2000. *A Year Down Yonder.* New York: Dial Books for Young Readers. Fresh phrases and hardworking verbs blend masterfully in this combination of poignant philosophy and wry humor. Superb dialogue can be used to teach sentence fluency and voice.

Pinkney, Andrea Davis. 1998. *Duke Ellington.* New York: Hyperion Books for Children. This selection features extraordinary and original use of nouns, verbs, and modifiers to create both mood and imagery.

Plourde, Lynn. 1999. *Wild Child.* New York: Simon & Schuster Books for Young Readers. This book uses quirky, playful language. Ideal for sparking interest in poetry or other imaginative writing.

Spandel, Vicki, with Ruth Nathan and Laura Robb. 2001. *Daybook of Critical Reading and Writing* (Grade 5 edition). Wilmington, MA: Great Source. A marvelous collage of reading and writing activities based on the most exceptional literature of our time.

Lights, Camera, Action!

For use with pages 58–62 in the Student Traitbook

This lesson emphasizes the importance of using *verbs* to energize writing. Action verbs enliven text, adding details that create a feeling of excitement or anticipation. Verbs are far more powerful than modifiers. One good verb can usually upstage a chorus of adjectives. Compare "The speaker felt *nervous, anxious, worried, uncomfortable,* and *unprepared*" (adjectives) to "The speaker *clenched* and *unclenched* her fists, *clutched* her notes, *fluffed* her hair for the tenth time, and *eyed* the clock—for it was almost time to begin" (action verbs).

Objectives

Students will become aware of strong verbs, practice comparing strong and weak verbs, and create original text containing strong verbs.

Skills Focus

- Listening and reading for strong verbs
- Identifying strong verbs
- Comparing two passages: one with weak verbs, one with strong verbs
- Discussing the power of verbs in writing
- Creating a piece of original writing that contains strong verbs

Time Frame

Allow 50 minutes for this lesson, excluding extension activities. You may divide the lesson by saving the writing activity (Directing Your Own Writing) for a separate lesson. You will then have two 25-minute lessons.

Setting Up the Lesson

Use the unit introduction on Student Traitbook page 58 to introduce word choice. This lesson depends heavily on students' understanding verbs so spend time discussing them. Because verbs are action words, they energize writing in a way that other words cannot. Precise nouns and colorful adjectives are important; however, nothing replaces the force of a powerful verb. You can illustrate this by revising a simple sentence containing an adjective. Use the overhead to show some examples:

Althea's **tired** feet hurt, but she climbed the **high** hill. (adjectives)
Althea **struggled, gasped, willed** her legs forward, and **ignored** the pain in her arches—but the top of the hill still **loomed** far in the distance. (verbs)

Marvin was **angry** about the mean note and showed his **strong** feelings. (adjectives)
Marvin **stomped** on the floor and **flushed** bright red as he **ripped** the note to shreds. (verbs)

After doing three or four such examples, you might ask your students to give you a simple sentence containing one adjective: *Veronica's room was* **messy.** *Cleaning the garage was* **hard.** *The turtle was* **slow.** Then, together, create a revision energized by strong **verbs.**

Teaching the Lesson

Sharing an Example:
A Year Down Yonder

Read aloud the excerpt on Student Traitbook page 60, asking students to follow along. It's a lively passage, energized by powerful verbs and an unforgettable portrait of Grandma Dowdel. Emphasize the verbs, all of which appear in color so that students can easily spot them as you read together.

After sharing the passage, ask students to identify favorite verbs and to describe the pictures those verbs made in their minds. Also, ask whether there are any verbs that students did not understand. Explain the meaning of any new verb. Are there any verbs that students would like to use in their own writing? This is a good time to introduce the concept of a personal dictionary: a place for storing new, favorite words. A personal dictionary is helpful because it is in a student's notebook and contains words that he or she wants to learn and use.

Writing Without the Action Words

Read the revised version of Richard Peck's original, which shows what happens when powerful verbs are replaced with dull substitutes. Again, remind students to pay attention to the words in color, which replace the words in the original.

Your Response

Make sure that students verbalize their comparisons between the two pieces and fill out the Your Response section. Most students will agree that the first version is much more engaging than the second. Ultimately, students should see that verbs affect imagery and mood. Verbs also bring out the writer's voice.

Spotting the Action Words

This portion of the lesson, on Student Traitbook page 61, reinforces what students have learned by having them revise a passage with no boldface clues. This time, they have to spot the verbs for themselves. They should find many strong verbs in the passage: *noticed, locked, scrambling, dodging, blast, deflected, ripped, streamed, slammed* and so on. If students are struggling, they need to read again. You may wish to review the definition of an action verb to make the search easier.

Share and Compare

Have students compare their work with partners. If students do not find all the verbs, point out those they missed. Remind students to add favorites to their personal dictionaries.

Directing Your Own Writing

As a prewriting activity, have students generate verb lists as they picture themselves in the situation each has chosen. For example, if a student has chosen to write about hitting the winning home run, the verb list might include *warming up, stretching, yelling, throwing the ball, listening, swinging the bat, sprinting,* or *reaching.* The student need not use all these verbs, but the list helps him or her focus and provides a word bank from which to draw. When students have finished, have them underline the strongest verbs and share paragraphs in response groups. Remind group members to listen closely for verbs and make note of them.

Extending the Lesson

- Keep a list of "Favorite Verbs" posted on the wall, adding to it as students suggest new entries.

- Continue to read aloud from pieces that have strong verbs and ask students to write down favorites. See the list of recommended books on page 60 of this Teacher's Guide.

- Notice when students use strong verbs, and use the code **SV** for **S**trong **V**erb.

Headline News— use Writer's clues!

For use with pages 63–66 in the Student Traitbook

Word *choice* implies that student writers have a personal collection of words from which to choose. One way to develop this personal word bank is through reading. Avid readers continually pick up new vocabulary words—but doing this requires a reader's trick: determining meaning from *context.* Readers must use the clues a writer provides, noticing just how the writer uses the word in a sentence or paragraph. Good readers may not be conscious of it, but they are routinely thinking to themselves, "This word *probably* means . . . ." How do they know? Because context provides the evidence.

Objectives

Students will understand how to use context to determine meaning. They will recognize the importance of adding new words to their personal word banks.

Skills Focus

- Understanding the concept of context
- Guessing at word meanings out of context
- Guessing at word meanings using context
- Confirming uncertain meanings by consulting a dictionary

Time Frame

Allow 35 minutes for this lesson.

Setting Up the Lesson

Students need to understand that seeing a word in context means seeing how it is used in a sentence. An unfamiliar word can be hard to define or understand. Put the word in context, though, and most readers can make an educated guess: *Ramona was so **persnickety** she wouldn't even drink a cup of tea or eat a piece of toast unless she had made it herself.* A reader who is thinking about context might say, "Well, Ramona won't eat or drink a thing unless she makes it herself—so **persnickety** can't mean easygoing or indifferent. It must mean ***fussy,*** right?"

Teaching the Lesson

Desert Island Words: *The Thief*

On Student Traitbook page 64, students discover how difficult it is to determine word meanings when words stand in isolation. That is what out of context means. Reassure them that this is NOT a test—it's a guessing game. They should make any guess at a word meaning that seems to fit. They are going to see these words again—but next time, the words will be used in context (in sentences). That will make part 2 of this guessing game much easier. For now, they should just relax and let their imaginations soar.

Putting Words Back in Context

Here students see the same words, but this time in context, as they were used in Megan Whelen Turner's *The Thief*. Students are still playing the guessing game, but now they have clues to help them. You can get them started, if you wish, by doing one of the words together as a class.

Try *ravine,* for example. Many students may know this one—and in that case, context clues will reaffirm what they know. If students do not recognize the word, encourage them to look carefully at the whole sentence. What clues does it offer? The ravine is deep, and it is part of a streambed. This suggests a steep gully or small canyon carved into the earth by the water. As you work on this example, talk through the "word problem" aloud. Tell students that talking to themselves, though it might feel a little silly at first, is often useful in coming up with definitions. Saying possible word meanings aloud will help them think through which ones make sense.

Discuss and Check

Go over *all* word meanings after students have finished guessing. Allow for some variety; there is more than one way to define each word. Help students by asking them to describe in their own words what a word might mean or what it reminds them of or what mental picture it creates. You can complete the definition process with the kind of verbalizing described earlier. Be sure to confirm all definitions with a dictionary check. You may wish to divide the work among several groups. That way, no one will have too many definitions to look up, and students will enjoy sharing what they find and letting others compare their guesses to actual meanings.

Extending the Lesson

- Continue the "in context" practice when you encounter other words your students do not know. Instead of providing a definition, write a line or two on the overhead, and ask them to guess meaning from context. With enough practice, this guessing becomes a habit.

- When you use a word that students do not recognize, encourage them to ask you to "put it in context"; in other words, "use it in a sentence." Do so, and see whether they can figure out the meaning from the way you use the word. Consider reversing the process occasionally!

- When you find an interesting word in your reading, consider sharing a line or two with students to see whether they can guess the correct meaning. Be sure to choose a word that is used correctly and clearly—one for which the writer has provided good context clues.

- Encourage students to introduce one new word into each piece of writing they create and to make the definition of the word clear from context. When students share, invite them to point out their context words.

Painting Word Pictures

For use with pages 67–70 in the Student Traitbook

Sensory language **helps readers see, hear, smell, taste, and touch every experience as if they were right there with the writer.** The wind glided like a feather across her cheeks as the tireless horse drove a path through the tall summer grass **is much more powerful than** She could feel the wind when the horse ran. **In the first example, we feel the wind on our faces and imagine the speed and power of the horse. The second example gives us facts without the feelings that would put us at the scene. When students learn the power of sensory language, they open their experience to readers.**

Objectives

Students will understand sensory language, identify such language, and use sensory language in their writing.

Skills Focus

- Learning the meaning of sensory language
- Identifying sensory details in a piece of writing
- Creating a sensory detail table as a form of prewriting
- Creating a piece of writing that includes sensory details

Time Frame

Allow 50 minutes for this lesson, excluding Extending the Lesson. You can divide it into two 25-minute lessons by using Your Turn—Be a Word Artist in the second lesson.

Setting Up the Lesson

Explain to students that **sensory details** are *any* details that appeal to the five senses: seeing, hearing, smelling, tasting, and touching. Ask students to imagine themselves at a favorite place: the county fair, an amusement park, the beach, the movies, or the kitchen at home. Tell them to list all the sights they can think of, then the sounds, then the smells, and so forth. Go through the five senses systematically. Students will notice different things, and that's good. You're creating a kind of impressionistic collage that shows students how many things there are to notice in their surroundings. List students' thoughts on the overhead. Then, ask whether students could write a description of this place with ALL these details.

Teaching the Lesson

Sharing an Example:
Homeless Bird

Homeless Bird is set in India. Some of your students may have visited this part of the world, but even if they have not, ask them to imagine how it might look, sound, feel, and smell to be there. Talk about this briefly, and then read the passage on Student Traitbook pages 67–68 to see how many impressions match.

Sensory Reaction

Students should first underline the sensory details they notice in Whelan's passage. Then they can compare what they noticed with the details shown in the sensory chart on page 68 of the Student Traitbook. Some students may underline more details than are shown in the chart. A reader may notice many more sensory details and have a far more vivid picture in his or her mind than could be created from the chart. Remind students that the chart is only a model, and encourage them to make even better charts in the next part of this lesson.

Your Own Table

This poem is light and funny; it is also full of sensory details that will appeal to many baseball fans. Remind students to underline details and then record what they find in the chart provided. They need not use every column or list every detail. Each student should easily find five or six details to list. Some will find more. Challenge students to list a variety of details—not all details should relate to sights or to sounds, for instance.

Your Turn—Be a Word Artist

This part of the lesson, on page 70 of the Student Traitbook, begins with a strong prewriting activity: listing sensory details. Let students know that this activity is a good strategy to use when they are writing descriptions.

Make a similar list yourself on an overhead transparency, but do not show it to students until their lists are finished. You do not want them to copy your list.

Make sure that students choose only one of the topics: hunger and food OR an experience in nature. Then they should decide whether to write a poem or a paragraph. Because a poem is often made up of phrases, the list of details accounts for about half of the poetry writer's work. (You may wish to keep this in mind when advising your writers. The paragraph is a little more challenging.) Remind poetry writers that poems do not have to rhyme. They need to search for the right word—not the rhyming word.

Share

When students have finished writing, allow them to share their writing in response groups or with the class. Explain how you used your prewriting list of details as the basis for your draft. If you left out some details or added others, point this out. Remind students that prewriting is meant to get the writer started. It should not restrict the writer to a preliminary list of details.

Extending the Lesson

- Share pieces of literature in which sensory details are strong, and ask students to tell you which ones they remember best. (See the list of suggested books on page 60 of this Teacher's Guide.) Make a list of these.

- With your students, generate a list of potential writing topics that lend themselves to use of sensory detail.

- Ask each student to write on ONE of the topics from your list (or to come up with another topic). You write, too. When students have finished, have them share their sensory detail papers and add them to their writing folders.

Brush Strokes, Not Buckets!

For use with pages 71–74 in the Student Traitbook

This lesson helps students understand that an important part of word choice is avoiding the use of too many words. Wordiness and repetition can smother the writer's message, impairing clarity. This lesson is particularly effective for students who have a tendency to write to fill space (even when they run out of ideas), or for those who may think that longer is better.

Objectives

Students will understand that concise, simple language enhances clarity and makes text more appealing. They will learn to identify redundancy and revise for wordiness.

Skills Focus

- Understanding the concept of clutter
- Assessing a piece of writing for wordiness
- Revising a wordy piece to make it concise

Time Frame

Allow about 40 minutes for this lesson, excluding Extending the Lesson activities. Students are asked to do two major revisions: one on "J.J. and Me: Friends or Twins?", and one on "How I Like to Spend My Time." You can, if you wish, divide this lesson into two 20-minute lessons, doing one revision activity in each.

Setting Up the Lesson

Sometimes more of a good thing is too much. You can illustrate this with a bucket and some rocks. Bring in a bucket and enough rocks to create a heavy load. Put *one* rock in the bucket and ask one of your students to lift it. Then add more rocks, one at a time. Ask the student to tell you when the bucket starts to feel heavy. This process illustrates that too much weight soon becomes uncomfortable. Point out that words have a "weight" of their own. Because readers need to process language quickly, wordiness and repetition quickly make reading a chore.

> *I try for motion in every paragraph. I hate sentences that begin, "There was a storm." Instead, write, "A storm burst."*
>
> —Barbara Tuchman

Teaching the Lesson

Sharing an Example:
J.J. and Me: Friends or Twins?

This sample on Student Traitbook pages 71–72 is wordy. It reads as though the writer cannot spit the words out fast enough. As a result, the main message—*J.J. and I have a lot in common*—is buried in verbiage. Read the passage aloud first, asking students to note the clutter.

Your Response

Make sure that students fill in this section. Then, each student should reread the section with a partner. Partners should decide together which words, sentences, or phrases can be cut without interfering with the writer's message. Encourage students to cut all the clutter they can find. Ask volunteers to read their revisions aloud.

Side by Side

Students have now revised the wordy paragraph by deleting clutter. Some students will cut very little. They may be fearful of cutting too much. Willingness to cut as much as necessary comes with practice.

Compare

Make sure that students fill in this section, noting how much they have cut compared to the revision. If they cut much less, encourage them to review their work and cut more.

As you compare revisions and have students read their revisions aloud, remember that students do *not* learn to revise in one lesson. Making writing concise is a skill students will work on throughout their lives. Begin slowly, keeping expectations reasonable, and repeat this lesson often to increase skill.

Cut the Clutter

Encourage students to cut any unnecessary information. The goal is to make the paragraph short and concise. If students have not cut *at least* 30 words, they have NOT cut enough. Ask them to try again. Fully half of this paragraph can be deleted.

Share and Compare

Encourage partners to compare and explain their deletions.

Extending the Lesson

- On the overhead, write a draft on any topic and deliberately make it wordy. Read the draft aloud, and have students rate it: very wordy, a little wordy, or not at all wordy. Ask for their help in identifying clutter, and let them guide you in making cuts.

- Ask each student to create a wordy piece for his or her partner to revise.

- Ask each student to look at a recent draft of his or her writing and delete all clutter.

- Make a wall chart, and ask students to rate themselves according to their skill at eliminating wordiness: 5—Ruthless, 3—Determined but still holding back a little, 1—Nervous about removing too many words.

Word Choice

Teacher's Guide pages 59, 156–167
Overhead numbers 13–16

Objective

Students will review and apply what they have learned about the trait of word choice.

Reviewing Word Choice

Review with students what they have learned about the trait of word choice. Ask students to discuss what word choice means and to explain why it is important in a piece of writing. Then ask them to recall the main points about word choice that are discussed in Unit 4. Students' responses should include the following points:

- Choose strong verbs.
- Use context to determine word meaning.
- Describe with sensory words.
- Delete unnecessary words.

Applying Word Choice

To help students apply what they have learned about the trait of word choice, distribute copies of the Student Rubric for Word Choice on page 59 of this Teacher's Guide. Students will use these to score one or more sample papers that can be found beginning on page 116. The papers for word choice are also on overheads 13–16.

Before students score the papers, explain that a rubric is a grading system to determine the score a piece of writing should receive for a particular trait. Preview the Student Rubric for Word Choice, pointing out that a paper very strong in word choice receives a score of 6, and a paper very weak in word choice receives a score of 1. Tell students to read the rubric and then to read the paper to be scored. Then tell them to look at the paper and rubric together to determine the score the paper should receive. Encourage students to make notes on each paper to help them score it. For example, they might put a checkmark nest to sentences in which a strong voice emerges..

Unit 5

Sentence Fluency

Overview

Sentence fluency is about the flow and rhythm of writing. Fluent writing has a cadence, a sound that's smooth, sometimes even lyrical. Fluent writing has a smooth, natural sound that is balanced with a variety of sentence lengths and beginnings.

The focus of the instruction in this unit will be

- modeling how to combine sentences for fluency
- making students aware of varying the length of sentences for variety
- encouraging students to use authentic-sounding dialogue
- having students practice revising fluency problems

Sentence Fluency: *A Definition*

Sentence fluency is the rhythm and flow of language, especially as that rhythm and flow enhance clarity. Passages strong in fluency are marked by noticeable variety in sentence length and structure, readily identifiable connections between sentences, and an absence of such problems as choppiness, repetitive sentence length, stiff or forced dialogue, and run-ons. Fluent writing is a pleasure to read aloud. Keep in mind that sentence *fluency* and sentence *structure* are not exactly the same. Although grammar plays a role in achieving fluency, this unit focuses more on sentence variety and readability than on grammatical correctness. Correctness falls under the trait of conventions.

The Unit at a Glance

The following lessons in the Teacher's Guide and practice exercises in the Student Traitbook will help develop understanding of the trait of sentence fluency. The Unit Summary provides an opportunity to practice evaluating papers for sentence fluency.

Unit Introduction: Sentence Fluency

Teacher's Guide pages 74–78
Student Traitbook page 75

Students are introduced to the unique features of sentence fluency.

Lesson 17: Rolling Like a River

Teacher's Guide pages 79–81
Student Traitbook pages 76–79

Students use the strategy of sentence combining to help eliminate the repetitive choppiness of short sentences.

Lesson 18: VARY Length—or Be VERY Boring!

Teacher's Guide pages 82–84
Student Traitbook pages 80–83

Students examine text and revise for sentence variety.

Lesson 19: Dynamite Dialogue

Teacher's Guide pages 85–87
Student Traitbook pages 84–87

Students assess a sample of dialogue and revise another sample to give it the natural sound of real conversation.

Lesson 20: Focusing on Fluency in Your Own Writing

Teacher's Guide pages 88–90
Student Traitbook pages 88–90

Students use what they have learned in the first three lessons, together with their assessment skills, to evaluate and revise a personal piece of writing for sentence fluency. As part of the lesson, they will read aloud in response groups.

Unit Summary: Sentence Fluency

Teacher's Guide page 91
Overhead numbers 17–20

Use the rubric on page 77 and the activities in the Summary to practice evaluating writing for sentence fluency.

Teacher Rubric for Sentence Fluency

6 • The writing is smooth, natural, and easy to read.
  • Virtually every sentence begins differently; sentences vary in length.
  • Dialogue, if used, sounds natural and conversational.
  • The piece invites expressive oral reading that brings out the voice.

5 • The writing is smooth and easy to read.
  • Many sentences begin differently; variety in sentence length is noticeable.
  • Dialogue, if used, sounds natural.
  • The piece is a good one for reading aloud.

4 • The writing is easy to read in most places. A few sentences are choppy.
  • Some sentences begin differently; there is some variety in sentence length.
  • Dialogue, if used, sounds reasonably natural, though a little stiff in places.
  • This piece could be read aloud with some rehearsal.

3 • The writing is sometimes easy to read. Choppy sentences, run-ons, or other problems may necessitate some rereading.
  • Sentence beginnings tend to be alike; sentences tend to be of equal length.
  • Dialogue, if used, rarely sounds conversational.
  • Rehearsal is needed before reading this piece aloud.

2 • Choppy sentences, run-ons, or other problems make the writing difficult to follow.
  • Many sentences begin the same way; most are of equal length.
  • Dialogue, if used, does not sound conversational.
  • This piece is hard to read aloud, even with rehearsal.

1 • The writing is consistently difficult to follow. Choppiness, run-ons, or other sentence problems abound.
  • Sentences consistently begin with the same word or phrase, or it is hard to tell *where* they begin. Sentence length may show little or no variation.
  • Dialogue, if used, is forced.
  • The piece is *very* difficult to read aloud, even with rehearsal.

Student Rubric for Sentence Fluency

6
- My writing is clear, smooth, and easy to read.
- Sentences begin in *many* different ways. My sentences range from long to very short.
- If I used dialogue, it sounds like real conversation.
- The reader will enjoy reading this paper out loud.

5
- My writing is clear and smooth most of the time. It's pretty easy to read.
- Most of my sentences begin in different ways and are of different lengths.
- If I used dialogue, I did a good job. It sounds real.
- I think the reader will enjoy reading this paper aloud. It sounds smooth.

4
- Some of my writing is smooth. It needs work here and there.
- Some sentences begin in different ways. I have SOME long or short sentences.
- If I used dialogue, I did fine. It sounds like real conversation.
- The reader can read this paper aloud with a little practice.

3
- This writing needs more fluency. I might have choppy sentences or run-ons.
- Many of my sentence beginnings are the same. Most of my sentences are the same length.
- If I used dialogue, it needs work. It doesn't sound like real conversation.
- It is not easy to read this paper aloud.

2
- This writing is hard to read! I have choppy sentences, run-ons, or other problems.
- Too many of my sentences begin the same way and are the same length.
- I do not think my dialogue sounds like real conversation. I'm not sure why.
- It is hard to read this aloud. It is even hard for me.

1
- This writing is very hard to read. I can't tell one sentence from another.
- It is hard to tell where my sentences begin. I'm not sure whether the beginnings are different or not. I'm not sure how long my sentences are.
- I am not sure whether this writing has dialogue.
- This is very hard to read aloud. I can't even do it.

Recommended Books for Teaching Sentence Fluency

Sentence fluency *must* be learned by listening, not just by reading and looking. As you share literature—strong or weak in sentence fluency— remember to ask your students questions like these: *Do you like the sound of this? Why or why not? What would you do to improve the fluency?*

Bedard, Michael. 1992. *Emily*. New York: Bantam Doubleday Dell. Wonderful dialogue and fluent, lyrical writing fill this fact-based story of poet Emily Dickinson.

Cisneros, Sandra. 1989. *The House on Mango Street*. New York: Random House. Prose that reads like poetry enhances this marvelous coming-of-age book. Select passages you enjoy and read them aloud.

Clinton, Catherine, ed. 1998. *I, Too, Sing America: Three Centuries of African American Poetry*. Boston: Houghton Mifflin. Excellent read-aloud poetry that fuses voice and fluency.

Fleischman, Paul. 1988. *Joyful Noise: Poems for Two Voices*. New York: HarperCollins. This selection features dialogue to make reader's theater come alive.

Gantos, Jack. 1997. *Jack's Black Book*. New York: Farrar, Straus and Giroux. Natural dialogue provides an opportunity for hilarious read-aloud, reader's theater.

Grimes, Nikki. 1999. *My Man Blue*. New York: Penguin Putnam. These poems invite dramatic reading, featuring sentence variety that's half dialogue, half music to the ear.

Kemper, Dave, with Ruth Nathan, Patrick Sebranek, and Carol Elsholz. 2000. *Writers Express: A Handbook for Young Writers, Thinkers, and Learners*. Wilmington, MA: Great Source. Writing process, writers' tips, connections to the six traits, forms of writing, proofreaders' guides—this selection features all the basics you need to bring the traits to life.

Paulsen, Gary. 1993. *Harris and Me*. New York: Bantam Doubleday Dell Publishing. This book has highly readable dialogue.

———. 1998. *Soldier's Heart*. New York: Bantam Doubleday Dell Publishing Group. This is a fact-based account of Charlie Goddard, a young soldier in the Civil War. It is rich in voice and fluency and is good for showing sentence variety and strong rhythmic prose.

Sachar, Louis. 1998. *Holes*. New York: Scholastic, Inc. A superb read-aloud book— select passages that show great sentence variety.

Rolling Like a River

For use with pages 75–79 in the Student Traitbook

Fluent writing moves with the rhythm and grace of a rolling river. Of course, just as a river can be dammed to block the flow of water, writing can suffer from obstacles that block the smooth flow of words. Repetitive, choppy sentence structure is a major obstacle to fluency: *We went hiking. The hills were high. It was fun. We liked it. It was sunny.* **Combining choppy sentences to create a smoother, easier flow is what this lesson is all about. Some sentences, of course, can and should remain short and forceful—and that is part of the lesson, too.**

Objectives

Students will combine sentences to create longer, more fluent sentences.

Skills Focus

- Listening for choppy sentences
- Selecting sentences that could be combined
- Combining sentences to improve fluency
- Reading "before" and "after" pieces aloud to contrast the change in fluency

Time Frame

Allow 30–35 minutes for this lesson.

Setting Up the Lesson

Use page 75 of the Student Traitbook to introduce the concept of sentence fluency. To illustrate the importance of fluent writing, write a brief anecdote from your own life, and share it with the class. Make each sentence very choppy and repetitive: *I went shopping. I went on Saturday. I looked for flowers. I like flowers. Geraniums are my favorites.* Ask students about this writing. Do they like it? How could it be improved? Let them know that choppiness is a problem you will work on in this lesson. If time permits, you can revise the anecdote and read the "before" and "after" versions aloud.

Teaching the Lesson

Sharing an Example: Sand Dune Adventure

Read aloud "Sand Dune Adventure" on Student Traitbook page 77, asking students to follow along. They should notice very quickly how choppy the writing is. They are asked to respond in two parts. First, under "Your Response," students should rate the overall flow; most probably will find it "full of starts and stops." Then, under "Can You Find the Problem?" students should identify *specifically* what is wrong. Most should easily recognize two problems: *The sentences sound short and choppy,* and *The writer does not put enough information into each sentence.* Emphasize that the one-idea-per-sentence approach to writing often leads to choppiness. Remind students, however, that some short sentences are acceptable. An *occasional* short sentence adds variety.

Revised Example: Sand Dune Adventure

Remind students to use their eyes and ears to compare the revision to the original choppy version. The revision is much smoother, but they should look and listen carefully to see whether they agree. Some students may wish to combine sentences in different ways or to leave some short sentences alone. Encourage these individual approaches. This is one revision; it is not the ONLY revision possible.

Combining: How to Do It

This section on Student Traitbook page 78 shows students how sentence combining works. Emphasize that the method is like addition in math. Each time you add a sentence, you get a slightly bigger sentence. It is different from math in one important way, however. Before explaining the difference see whether students can figure it out. In math, if you add 5 + 5, you always get 10. In writing, on the other hand, you could add one 5-word sentence to another and come up with an 8-word combination. Explain also that writers often add connecting words to newly combined sentences to show how ideas are related.

Let's Get Rolling!

Students will analyze a piece of writing, "The Giving Garden," to see which sentences could be combined to increase sentence fluency. Read the passage aloud while students listen. As an alternative, ask a volunteer to read aloud.

Revise

After students have heard the passage read aloud, have them reread it silently. Ask them to put plus signs (+) between two or more sentences that can be combined. They may also wish to put numbers (2, 3, and so on) above each choppy sentence that will begin a new big sentence. This will help them avoid confusion when they're revising.

Be sure that students read their revisions aloud to see how well they have done.

Extending the Lesson

- Ask students to choose a fluent piece and revise it so that all the sentences begin in the same way. Have volunteers present their "before" and "after" pieces to the class.

- Invite students to create choppy pieces of writing that include from six to eight sentences. Then, have them exchange papers with partners to see whether partners can improve the flow.

- Ask volunteers to read their revisions of "The Giving Garden" aloud. Ask listeners to comment on the fluency. Read your own revision aloud, as well. You may wish to give students printed copies of your "before" and "after" versions.

VARY Length— or Be VERY Boring!

For use with pages 80–83 in the Student Traitbook

Good writers avoid creating sentences that are all the same length. They know that variety in sentence length promotes smooth, fluid writing. Fluent writing interweaves long, complete sentences with occasional short, crisp remarks. Variety keeps readers alert and interested.

Objectives

Students will notice sentence length in their own or others' writing, and they will revise to vary sentence length.

Skills Focus

- Noticing when too many sentences are the same length
- Identifying revision strategies that help create variety in length
- Applying some or all of those strategies to revise text in which sentence lengths do not vary

Time Frame

Allow 35–40 minutes for this lesson, excluding Extending the Lesson activities. If you prefer, turn this into two lessons by saving the section called "Time to Revise: Vary the Length" for Lesson 2. You will then have two 20-minute lessons, with the actual revision practice in Lesson 2.

Setting Up the Lesson

Ask students how long their sentences usually are. They can simply estimate the number of words or use a more methodical approach. For the latter, ask the students to look at a short piece of writing they have done recently and to count the words in each sentence. What is the shortest sentence? What is the longest sentence? What is the average? (Divide the total number of words by the total number of sentences.) Who writes the shortest sentences in the class? Who writes the longest? Explain that actual length isn't as important as variety. In fluent writing, both long and short sentences are effective.

> *When I see a paragraph shrinking under my eyes like a strip of bacon in a skillet, I know I'm on the right track.*
>
> —Peter de Vries

Teaching the Lesson

Sharing an Example: *The View from Saturday*

This is extraordinarily fluent writing. As you read it aloud, most students should note great variety in sentence lengths. The passage opens with an extremely long sentence that piles idea on idea—but the passage ends with an equally effective six-word sentence. Ask students whether that closing sentence would have as much energy if *all* the sentences were about six words long.

Your Response

Make sure that students rate the passage. Then see whether they are surprised by the actual numbers. Would they have guessed that the first sentence contained 59 words?

Your Turn to VARY Sentences

The example in this section is in serious need of revision. Most of the sentences are exactly six words long, and only two vary slightly from that number. As you read the piece, you will not have to exaggerate to make it sound choppy. Ask students to respond orally to the piece. How does it sound? Do they hear much variety in sentence length?

Do the Numbers

Have students "Do the Numbers" by actually counting the words and filling in the spaces. Review the list of revision strategies with students to be sure that each strategy is clear. Answer questions about any strategy that seems unclear, and model it if necessary. You may also wish to ask students which strategies they have used previously to revise for fluency. This discussion will help to prepare students for the revision task that is the key portion of this lesson.

Time to Revise: Vary the Length

Here students revise the piece, using strategies from the list or any other ideas they develop on their own. The goal is to introduce variety into the suitcase passage and to create writing that has a smooth and rhythmic sound when read aloud.

Share and Compare

Make sure that students work individually before sharing their revisions with partners. You may also wish to have volunteers read their revised pieces to the class so that you can hear some different approaches to revision.

Extending the Lesson

- Continue practice by asking students to count words in just one paragraph of any textbook. Do they find any sentence variety? If not, have them revise to improve the flow.

- Ask volunteers to create short passages in which sentences are varied in length—or not varied at all. They should not reveal which approach they are taking. Then, have volunteers read their passages aloud, and have listeners comment on what they hear. Are students able to pick out the pieces that have variety by listening?

- Go back to the piece of personal writing that students analyzed to prepare for this lesson. Ask students whether they can improve the variety in sentence length by combining sentences and varying sentence beginnings.

- Suppose Sentence Fluency and Choppy Writing were two characters who could have a talk. What might they say to each other? Ask students to create a short dialogue between the two, mimicking the way each one might discuss good writing, doing an assignment, selecting a favorite book or poem, improving punctuation, or any similar topic.

Dynamite Dialogue

For use with pages 84–87 in the Student Traitbook

Many students enjoy incorporating *dialogue* into their writing, but they sometimes forget that written conversations are effective only when they sound like real people talking. Phony dialogue does little to tell about the characters or advance the plot.

> "Look out," said Bill. "The light is red. You must stop."
>
> "Oh, yes," said Ryan. "I know that rule. Red is for stop. Green is for go."

These characters sound like wind-up toys, not real people, and so we soon lose interest. We might be more interested if they sounded like this:

> "Stop! It's red!" Bill yelled. "Are you asleep or what?"
>
> "I see it. I see it. Stop yelling," Brian responded— knowing all the time he hadn't seen it. "Are you trying to break my eardrums?"

Objectives

Students will use dialogue effectively by making it sound like real conversation.

Skills Focus

- Assessing dialogue for authenticity
- Revising dialogue to make it sound authentic

Time Frame

Allow 35 minutes for this lesson.

Setting Up the Lesson

If you ask your students to define *dialogue*, many of them will probably say, "It's two people talking." This definition is not incorrect, but it is incomplete. Dialogue is a record of two people responding to each other and to their situation. Dialogue should be like verbal catch. One person "catches" what the other has thrown to him or her, then tosses back a remark that follows naturally.

To introduce this lesson, you may choose to read the two samples from the previous page. Ask students which conversation sounds more like two friends talking about crossing against the light. You may also choose to read a strong example of dialogue from a book. (See the list of recommended titles on page 78 of this Teacher's Guide). As you share samples, ask students to tell you whether the characters sound like real people and to tell what they learn about the characters from the way the characters speak. Point out that dialogue often reveals a character's mood and provides clues to the sort of person he or she is. Good dialogue should have a purpose. It can set a mood, tell us what a character is like, or show what is happening in a story.

Teaching the Lesson

Sharing an Example: *Heads or Tails*

Expression helps bring out the realism of this excellent piece on pages 84–85 of the Student Traitbook. This sample is a good one for reader's theater. Ask volunteers to read the piece aloud or to perform it. Performing brings dialogue to life and helps students understand why dialogue must be realistic and engaging.

Your Response

Can students tell from the dialogue how the dad feels? Can they tell how Jack feels? If so, you know that the writer has done a good job of making these characters sound real.

Real Conversation, Dynamite Dialogue

Jack Gantos brings his characters to life with the dialogue from *Heads or Tails* on pages 84–85 of the Student Traitbook. It's a different story with the conversation between Tessa and her dad (page 86). Their conversation does not sound realistic. Again, try to put energy into your reading, and then invite volunteers to do a dramatic reading of the converstion between Tessa and her dad. When you have completed the readings, talk about this dialogue. Does this conversation sound authentic? Why or why not? Be sure students mark their responses in the space indicated.

A Plan to Follow: From Dud to Dynamite!

Each student will work with a partner to rewrite the dialogue between Tessa and her dad. It is not necessary for students to follow the same conversation that appears in the sample. Tessa and her dad can discuss anything at all. Students should focus on trying to make a conversation sound realistic. When students are finished, have them read their revised dialogues aloud. Each student should read his or her character's lines.

> **Note:** *This is not a lesson in conventions, so do not put too much emphasis on correct punctuation of dialogue. Punctuation is important, but we do not want students' attention distracted from the primary task of making the dialogue sound authentic.*

Extending the Lesson

- Have each student write a dialogue between himself or herself and a character from a book. The dialogue should run at least ten lines (five lines for each character) and can be about anything at all.

- Have students write an additional dialogue between Jack and his dad or between Tessa and her dad. Set up a new situation in which Tessa and her dad go to the rodeo or buy some food that the other person does not like. Jack and his dad might go bike riding together. Tell students to have fun but to make the characters *real*.

- Ask students to think of a situation in which people have conversations. Have students think of a story to tell about one of these situations. Ask students to write the whole story in dialogue, showing what is happening by what people say. The story can be very simple and very short.

- Teach a related conventions lesson, showing students how to use paragraphs, quotation marks, periods, commas, semicolons, and so on in setting up dialogue.

Focusing on Fluency in Your Own Writing

For use with pages 88–90 in the Student Traitbook

This lesson offers students an opportunity to use what they have learned about fluency to revise a piece of their own writing. You may wish to have them assess the piece both before and after revision, using their Student Rubric for Sentence Fluency. (See page 77 of this Teacher's Guide.)

Objectives

Students will practice self-assessment and will revise a piece of personal writing.

Skills Focus

- Selecting a personal piece of writing that needs revision in fluency
- Assessing fluency in a personal piece of writing
- Reviewing various strategies for improving fluency
- Revising a piece for fluency

Time Frame

Allow 35–45 minutes for this lesson, excluding Extending the Lesson activities. Because the lesson involves both selecting and revising a piece of writing, you can break the lesson into two sessions, selecting papers one day and having students work on their revisions the next.

Setting Up the Lesson

This lesson asks students to revise a personal piece of writing for sentence fluency. Write a paragraph with some weaknesses in sentence fluency. Explain to students that you have chosen this piece to revise, and read it aloud. Ask them for suggestions on how to make it more fluent, and make a list of their suggestions.

> I don't have a very clear idea of who the characters are until they start talking.
>
> —Joan Didion

Teaching the Lesson

Select a Sample

Students will choose a piece of writing that needs to be revised to improve sentence fluency. Allow sufficient time for this activity. Suggest that each student look for a piece that

- sounds choppy when read aloud.

- has too many sentences the same length.

- has too many sentences that begin the same way.

- has dialogue that does not sound realistic.

Share, Compare, Read, and Discuss

Have students form small groups of three or four. Keep in mind students' need to feel comfortable during this process. Avoid putting "best friends" in the same group because this sometimes causes students to be less candid in their comments.

Discuss the roles of responder and writer on page 89 of the Student Traitbook.

Time to Revise

Review the list of revision possibilities with students, and suggest that they check those they plan to use. Some students will check all four possibilities. That is fine, but it is also helpful to set priorities so that students have a place to begin. Suggest that they star one or two strategies to focus on first. That way, they will not be overwhelmed by the size of the task. Revision is often most effective when it occurs in stages. If you think that your students will benefit from extra time, wait a day after the first round of revision, and let students take a second look later. Revising more than once may seem strange to many students, but it is common among professional writers, who may revise a piece many times.

Extending the Lesson

- Brainstorm the strategies students used most often. Have them discuss what was helpful in making their writing fluent.

- Invite volunteers to read their revisions aloud.

- Ask students to find favorite poems and to read them aloud. Have them listen to the rhythm.

- Invite several students to bring in examples of music that they think are good examples of fluency. Play 3–5 songs with especially good rhythm or lyrics that seem fluent. You can review the music before presenting it to the class. Bring a sample of your own to add to the collection.

Sentence Fluency

Teacher's Guide pages 77, 168–180
Overhead numbers 17–20

Objective

Students will review and apply what they have learned about the trait of sentence fluency.

Reviewing Sentence Fluency

Review with students what they have learned about the trait of sentence fluency. Ask students to discuss what sentence fluency means and to explain why it is important in a piece of writing. Then ask them to recall the main points about sentence fluency that are discussed in Unit 5. Students' responses should include the following points:

- Combine sentences for fluency.
- Vary sentence length.
- Use dialogue that sounds natural.
- Revise for fluency.

Applying Sentence Fluency

To help students apply what they have learned about the trait of sentence fluency, distribute copies of the Student Rubric for Sentence Fluency on page 77 of this Teacher's Guide. Students will use these to score one or more sample papers that can be found beginning on page 116. The papers for sentence fluency are also on overheads 17–20.

Before students score the papers, explain that a rubric is a grading system to determine the score a piece of writing should receive for a particular trait. Preview the Student Rubric for Sentence Fluency, pointing out that a paper that reads very smoothly receives a score of 6, and a paper that does not read at all smoothly receives a score of 1. Tell students to read the rubric and then to read the paper to be scored. Then tell them to look at the paper and the rubric together to determine the score the paper should receive. Encourage students to make notes on each paper to help them score it. For example, they might underline repetitive sentence beginnings or put an X next to run-on sentences.

Overview

In this unit, students build their knowledge of conventions. They will learn to distinguish between revising (making major changes in the message) and editing (correcting errors in conventions). Understanding what each of these processes requires helps students perform both with greater efficiency and purpose. This unit encourages students to assume responsibility for their own editing. In the process of becoming independent editors, students learn to use both their eyes and their ears to correct errors in conventions. Students will learn to recognize, interpret, and use eight editors' marks. They will work as professional editors do, identifying errors in faulty text and marking the text for correction.

The focus of the instruction in this unit will be

- making sure that students can distinguish between revising and editing
- giving students practice in searching for errors
- modeling the use of editors' marks to correct faulty text
- allowing students to edit their own work

Conventions: *A Definition*

Successfully implementing the trait of conventions includes using correct spelling, punctuation, grammar, and capitalization. The goals are that students will become skilled, independent editors and that they will learn to use conventions as a way to clarify meaning and enhance voice.

The Unit at a Glance

The following lessons in the Teacher's Guide and practice exercises in the Student Traitbook will help develop understanding of the trait of conventions. The Unit Summary provides an opportunity to practice evaluating papers for conventions.

Unit Introduction: Conventions

Teacher's Guide pages 92–96
Student Traitbook page 91

Students are introduced to the concept of conventions.

Lesson 21: Burgers, Granola Bars, Revising, and Editing

Teacher's Guide pages 97–99
Student Traitbook pages 92–95

Students explore the differences between revising and editing by studying examples and reviewing the writing changes required for each process.

Lesson 22: Developing Your Editor's Eye

Teacher's Guide pages 100–103
Student Traitbook pages 96–99

Students practice identifying errors and counting the number and types of errors they find.

Lesson 23: Clang the Symbols!

Teacher's Guide pages 104–107
Student Traitbook pages 100–102

Students are introduced to eight editors' marks and begin using them to make corrections in faulty text.

Lesson 24: Editing Is the Name of the Game

Teacher's Guide pages 108–111
Student Traitbook pages 103–105

Students will use their eyes, ears, and knowledge of editors' marks to identify and mark errors in two sample texts.

Unit Summary: Conventions

Teacher's Guide page 112
Overhead numbers 21–24

Use the rubric on page 95 and the activities in the Summary to practice evaluating writing for clear and correct use of conventions.

Teacher Rubric for Conventions

6
- The paper is virtually error-free.
- The writer uses conventions skillfully to clarify meaning.
- The writer shows control over a wide range of conventions for this grade level.
- This piece is virtually ready to publish.

5
- The paper contains a few minor errors.
- The writer often uses conventions to clarify meaning.
- The writer shows control over many conventions appropriate for this grade level.
- This piece is ready to publish with minor changes.

4
- Several minor errors; these errors do not impair meaning.
- The writer uses conventions with enough skill to keep the text readable.
- The writer shows control over many conventions appropriate for this grade level.
- Some editing is needed before publication.

3
- Noticeable, distracting errors *begin* to make the text hard to follow or understand.
- Errors are sufficiently serious to impair readability in spots.
- The writer knows some conventions, but he or she is not yet in control of them.
- Thorough, careful editing is needed before publication.

2
- Many serious errors make this text hard to follow.
- Serious errors consistently impair readability.
- This writer appears to know a few conventions, but he or she is not in control of them.
- Line-by-line editing is required before publication.

1
- Serious, frequent errors make this text very difficult to read or understand.
- The reader must search to find conventions that are handled correctly.
- This writer does not appear in control of many conventions appropriate for this grade level.
- Careful, word-by-word editing is required for publication.

Student Rubric for Conventions

6
- My paper has no errors that I can see or hear.
- I used conventions to clarify my message.
- I checked my spelling, punctuation, and grammar.
- This is ready to publish.

5
- The reader *might* find a few errors, but not many.
- I think my conventions help make my message clear.
- I checked my spelling, punctuation, and grammar. They are pretty good.
- I looked for mistakes. I found a couple. My paper is *almost* ready to publish.

4
- The reader will probably notice some errors. I need to edit more carefully.
- My message is clear.
- My spelling, punctuation, and grammar are *mostly* correct.
- This needs some careful editing before it's ready to publish.

3
- I have too many errors. The reader needs to slow down to read this.
- I did some things correctly. Still—I'm not sure my message is always clear.
- When I read this, I see a lot of errors in my spelling, punctuation, and grammar.
- This could use a lot of editing. It is not ready to publish.

2
- I have a lot of errors. This is very hard to read.
- I did a few things correctly, but mistakes make it hard to understand what I'm saying.
- I made way too many errors in my spelling, punctuation, and grammar.
- I need to edit this *line by line* before I publish it.

1
- I made so many mistakes I can hardly read this myself.
- It is hard to find things done correctly. It is hard to tell what my message is.
- I need to read this aloud, go over it more than once, and get help from a partner.
- I need to edit this *word by word* before I publish it.

Recommended Literature for Teaching Conventions

No book list is included with this set of lessons because virtually any book can be used to help teach conventions. Sections from students' favorite books are ideal for talking about writers' skills in using conventions and also about how conventions help bring out meaning. Conventions are more than a set of rules to be memorized; it is the meaning behind the convention that counts.

You will find many lessons, strategies, explanations, and tips to help students work successfully with **conventions** in the following Great Source handbook:

Kemper, Dave, with Ruth Nathan, Patrick Sebranek, and Carol Elsholz. 2000. *Writers Express: A Handbook for Young Writers, Thinkers, and Learners.* Wilmington, MA: Great Source.

Daily practice in identifying and correcting errors can be found in the following Great Source products:

Sebranek, Pat, and Dave Kemper. 2000. *Writers Express Daily Language Workouts* (grade 5). Wilmington, MA: Great Source.

Vail, Neil J., and Joseph F. Papenfuss. 2000. *Daily Oral Language* (grade 5). Wilmington, MA: Great Source.

Burgers, Granola Bars, Revising and Editing

For use with pages 91–95 in the Student Traitbook

This lesson is intended to help students understand the difference between *revising* and *editing*. By studying examples and looking carefully at the changes editors make to writing, students will learn their own definitions for these two important parts of the writing process.

Objectives

Students will understand the differences between revising and editing so that they can do each with greater purpose and efficiency.

Skills Focus

- Discussing the steps of revising and editing
- Examining the kinds of changes writers make to writing
- Deciding whether changes are examples of revising or editing
- Creating personal definitions for revising and editing

Time Frame

Allow about 30 minutes for this lesson. Actual writing time (except Extending the Lesson activities) is short. Students spend most of their time examining changes to text and creating definitions for revising and editing.

Setting Up the Lesson

Throughout this lesson, students will develop personal definitions for *revising* and *editing.* They should recognize that revising and editing are not the same. Use Student Response book page 91 to help introduce the concepts.

Here's an example that will further illustrate the difference between the two words: Your family is set to leave on a vacation to Hawaii. Everyone is excited. At the last minute, your family decides . . . to go to Australia instead! Is that a big change or a small one? Is it more like a "revision" of your vacation, or "editing"? Now let's say you're set to go to Hawaii when you remember that you've forgotten to lock your suitcase, so you take care of that detail. Is that "revision" of the vacation or "editing"? You do not need to answer these questions for students, and they do not need to answer them yet. Ask them to keep the examples in mind as they work through the lesson.

Teaching the Lesson

First Impressions: What Do You Remember?

Encourage students to write these definitions quickly (Student Traitbook page 92). This is not a test, and students can change their minds as they work through this lesson. Their definitions may change only a little, or they may change dramatically.

When students have finished writing, they should discuss their definitions with partners and then with the class. If it is helpful, record some first thoughts on chart paper, on an overhead transparency, or on the board.

All Together Now

In this part of the lesson, students create two lists of what writers and editors do to a piece of writing to create a final draft. As students brainstorm, they should decide whether each example they think of belongs in the **Revising** list or the **Editing** list. The idea is to create two lists of very different kinds of changes. You want students to see that although revising and editing have much in common, they are not exactly alike.

Your Response

Invite students to look again at their "first thoughts" to see whether their thinking has changed now that the class has made lists of what writers do.

Revising and Editing in Action

If the concepts of revising and editing are clear to students, the examples on page 94 of the Student Traitbook should be easy to label. **Sample 1** is clearly an example of revision. The writer has reversed the order of the steps related to recycling and has added information. These changes are part of revision.

Sample 2 is an example of editing. The writer has not changed the main ideas or the order of ideas, but he or she has corrected spelling, inserted missing words, fixed the punctuation, and so on. Students should see the two versions of Sample 2 as nearly identical except for the errors. If they do not, ask them to listen as you read each version aloud. They sound alike, except for missing words. That is not the case with the two versions of Sample 1.

Final Chance to Narrow It Down

By now, students should have a clear idea of the major differences between revising and editing. Therefore, the final checklist should not prove difficult: 1 = Revising (the lead is reworded and lengthened, and the voice changes as well as the information), 2 = Revising (sentences are reworked and reworded),

3 = Editing (only one word is changed), 4 = Revising (the entire conclusion is rewritten), and 5 = Editing (the writer is checking for capital letters, not altering meaning).

Student partners should compare answers before the class discussion. Elicit student responses before providing the answers. Ask students to support and explain their decisions.

Extending the Lesson

- Students can work as a group or in teams to write definitions of revising and editing for a poster to be displayed in class. Ask them to create definitions that would be useful to a new writer.

- In addition to the definitions posters, ask students to keep running lists of the kinds of changes they make when they revise or edit. Tell them to change or add to these lists as often as their understanding grows.

- Put a piece of text on the overhead, and make some changes to it. Ask students to tell you whether you are revising or editing.

Developing Your Editor's Eye

For use with pages 96–99 in the Student Traitbook

In this lesson, students develop a sharp "editor's eye" for finding writing errors. Students will count errors, mark text, and compare work with partners in an effort to increase their efficiency in spotting mistakes. *Note:* Students will be introduced to eight editors' marks in Lesson 23. You may wish to introduce the chart of editors' marks for use with Lesson 22. However, the focus of this lesson is primarily on encouraging students to *spot* errors.

Objectives

Students will see that practice increases their ability to spot errors.

Skills Focus

- Looking for errors
- Marking errors
- Identifying strategies for developing a sharp editor's eye
- Comparing personal editing with that of a partner

Time Frame

Allow about 35 minutes for this lesson.

Setting Up the Lesson

Because this lesson is about spotting errors, begin by showing students a piece of text that contains from one to three errors. This way, you challenge your students to look for errors that are not easy to find. If you cannot find a good example in a newspaper or magazine, write one yourself. Enlarge the piece and put it on the overhead. Then see how quickly students can spot the error(s). Commend them for having a good editor's eye when they find the errors. This type of exercise is an excellent way to open any editing practice lesson, so return to it often.

> *I love the flowers of afterthought.*
> —Bernard Malamud
> (speaking of the process of revision)

Teaching the Lesson

A Little Warm-Up
Here, students have a chance to scan the text on Student Traitbook page 96 to see how many errors they can spot. Encourage them to read the material more than once and then to check with partners.

A Quick Count and Share
Go through the text sentence by sentence as a class. On the board, keep a running tally of the number of mistakes that students have found. Here is the corrected text with nine errors marked in boldface:

I don't **know** what happened, but the end of the school year just sneaked up behind me and gave **me** a kick. **W**here did the **t**ime go**?** **I** guess I don't understand people who say **that** the school **[delete .]** year moves slowly.

A Magnifying Glass for Your Editor's Eye

This section on Student Traitbook page 97 shows some strategies editors use to improve their speed and accuracy. Encourage students to share their own ideas, too. Six helpful tips are listed in this section, and students have space to add their own strategies. You may wish to have students write their hints either individually or with a partner, and then have them share with the class.

Editor's Eyes Open: Ready, Set, Spot!

On Student Traitbook page 98, students will mark a longer piece of writing with many errors. Read the passage slowly because students will be circling errors as they spot them. Then, encourage students to read the text again to catch any errors they missed the first time.

Share and Compare

Students should compare with their editing partners to see how many errors they found, whether they found the same errors, and whether they used the same editors' marks. Then, review the entire piece as a class.

On page 103 is the corrected version with corrections marked in boldface. Words or punctuation marks that should be deleted appear in brackets. You may wish to enlarge this text and make an overhead to share with students, or you can go through the errors orally, noting each as you go. Be sure to explain any corrections that students do not understand.

Extending the Lesson

- Ask students to mark and correct the samples from this lesson. Then review the pieces with them to be sure corrections are accurate and inclusive.

- Ask students to look at magazines and newspapers to see whether they can find errors—this a great way to sharpen that editor's eye!

- Ask student partners to work together to present an editing lesson to the class: a sentence containing from one to three errors. They can print the sentence on the board or overhead and lead the class in a discussion of which errors the sentence contains and how to correct them.

My family is leaving for Italy on **F**riday. It will be the longest **trip** I have ever taken and my first trip out of the **c**ountry. We're flying into the city of **F**lorence and then driving into the countryside to stay in a house. I'm a little nerv**o**us because **I** don't speak Italian. I will try my best to learn some basic words to be polite and show them I'm trying. **M**y plan [**e**] is to keep a journal, take lots of pictures, and send postcards to all my friends. Ciao! (That's Italian for good-bye and sounds like "chow"!)

Clang the Symbols!

For use with pages 100–102 in the Student Traitbook

In this lesson, students are introduced to eight *editors' marks.* Introduce these symbols as a kind of editor's language: symbols are the way editors talk to each other or to writers about the mistakes in a piece of writing. Why use symbols? Think how cumbersome it would be if an editor had to write a little note about each error: "Insert quotation marks here to show dialogue." Two carets with quotation marks tucked inside say the same thing in less space.

Objectives

Students will learn eight commonly used editors' marks and apply them to faulty text.

Skills Focus

- Interpreting editors' marks
- Recalling what each mark means
- Using editors' marks to correct text
- Comparing personal text with that of an editing partner

Time Frame

Allow about 40 minutes for this lesson.

Setting Up the Lesson

Because this is a lesson about symbols, you may wish to ask students what kinds of symbols people commonly use to shorten communication time. One example is the "thumbs-up" sign. Just about everyone agrees that this means "Things are looking good!" Think about other symbols of communication: nodding your head, winking, rolling your eyes, waving, raising one eyebrow. Clearly, symbols are useful communication shortcuts. Can you think of others?

Teaching the Lesson

Eight Editors' Marks

Discuss each symbol in the chart on Student Traitbook page 101. The chart shows one example of each symbol, but that may not be enough. Use each symbol two or three times in various examples to show what each means.

A Little Warm-Up

In this warm-up activity, students are not asked to correct text. They will look at the marks another editor has inserted into faulty text and "read" each mark to see whether they can interpret the editor's message. Each student should work independently first and then compare interpretations with a partner. Finally, go over the answers, which are on page 106.

Be sure that student partners check to see that they "read" the editor's marks the same way. Ask students for their interpretations before giving them the answers.

You're the Editor, So Clang the "Symbols"!

Ask students to use editor's marks to edit the copy called "Graduation Day" on Student Traitbook page 102. They can refer to the chart as often as necessary. Remind students that they will not rewrite the paragraph. They are simply marking the text for someone else to fix.

Ask each student to work with a partner. Be sure students tell you which errors they spotted and which marks they used. You can use the corrected version (page 107) on the overhead and go through the errors individually.

Extending the Lesson

- Ask each student to check a piece of his or her own writing that is ready to publish. Then have students identify any errors, using the eight editors' marks. Finally, have students make the corrections.

- Make a class chart of editors' marks in very large print, and post them where everyone can refer to them easily.

- Ask students to serve as editing coaches for younger students who are about to publish their work.

ˇ"I donˇ't think I can go ˇSamane said⊙

The upside-down carets with the quotation marks indicate actual speech: *I don't think I can go.* The upside-down caret in the word *don't* indicates that an apostrophe needs to be inserted because this is a contraction. The caret with a comma indicates insertion of a comma after the word *go.* The period inside a circle shows the need for a period at the end of the sentence.

she won't ~~Need~~ **to** bring a coat.

The three lines under the lowercase *s* show that this first letter of the sentence needs to be capitalized. The slash through the letter N in *Need* shows that this capital should be a lowercase letter. The caret between *need* and *bring* and the word *to* above the line mean that the word *to* should be inserted.

My brothers need to ~~the~~ wash the car, mow the lawn, and sweep the driveway.

The delete symbol through the word *the* indicates that this word should be cut. The carets with commas after the words *car* and *lawn* indicate the need for commas to break up the series in the sentence.

My older brother **g**raduated from high school last night. One of the speakers said, **"**Your actions will speak volumes about your character.**"** I think she meant that people show who they are by **what** they do. **T**hat was a pretty good message. There were three other **s**peakers who seemed to go on forever, and I can't remember what they **said.** My brother and his friends sure looked relieved **and** happy when they picked up their diplomas.

Editing Is the Name of the Game

For use with pages 103–105 in the Student Traitbook

An editor's tools include a quick eye, a sharp ear, a pen or pencil, and a list of editors' marks. Editors also need confidence and the ability to identify errors. Confidence and ability come from practice, and that is what this lesson is about.

Objectives

Students will use their editing skills to edit their own writing.

Skills Focus

- Recalling editors' marks
- Identifying errors in faulty text
- Marking faulty text with editors' marks
- Working with a partner to determine how thorough personal editing has been

Time Frame

Allow about 40 minutes for this lesson, excluding Extending the Lesson. You can break this into two short lessons by doing the first editing practice ("Getting Revved Up") in one lesson and the second ("A Little More to Do") in another lesson. You will then have two 20-minute lessons.

Setting Up the Lesson

Start by writing a few editors' marks on the overhead or board, and ask students to identify them. Next, write short sentences with one or two errors to be corrected in each. Ask students to identify the errors and tell you what marks to use to correct them. Then make corrections, and ask students whether you have corrected all the errors (make one or two mistakes on purpose). Are students completely comfortable with the editing process? Ask how many enjoy editing. Positive feelings usually improve accuracy! Point out that students may use an editors' marks poster or checklist, including the list from Lesson 23, throughout this lesson.

Teaching the Lesson

Getting Revved Up

Students should use their eyes, ears, and knowledge of editors' marks for this portion of the lesson on Student Traitbook pages 103–104. Remind them to read the piece aloud so that they can hear errors as well as see them. Suggest that students read through the sample more than once.

Share and Compare

Students should check with partners to see how many errors each found and then to see whether each found the same errors. Ideally, students' individual error totals should be close! They should find 14 errors. The corrected version is on page 111.

A Little More to Do

Once again, suggest this approach: students should read aloud the text on Student Traitbook page 105 individually, pencils in hand. They should then read silently to themselves, marking any errors they missed the first time. Remind students to use editors' marks and to refer to a class checklist or to the list in Lesson 23. They should not check with partners until all personal editing is complete.

Share and Compare

Now student partners can determine whether they found the same errors. When comparisons are completed, do a survey to see which teams found the most errors. Be careful of zealous editors who may go over the limit! You may wish to talk about the difference between editing for style ("I'd like to say this a different way") and editing for correctness ("This is an error"). Students should spot 16 errors.

On page 111 is the corrected version, with corrections marked in boldface. Be sure to go over *each error* with your students to be sure that everyone understands why and how each mistake should be marked.

Extending the Lesson

- Create a poster-sized checklist that includes from six to eight kinds of editing problems your class will work to master. Do not let the list get longer than this for now. You can expand or change it as students develop their skills.

- Have students assess for errors in conventions. Assessing for errors in conventions is not only about finding errors. It is also important to notice what writers do well. Ask your students to identify some of the things their favorite authors do especially well. In addition, students may find some examples that could use improvement.

- Ask students to generate editing lessons for the entire class to work on, using the samples from Lesson 24 as models. Their lessons should contain no more than five or six sentences and no more than one or two errors per sentence. Students may wish to work with partners.

I thought **s**ummer was supposed to be a [**the**] time of relaxation. **M**y dad always says, "Summer, the way I remember it, is all about kids**,** bikes**,** families**,** sun**,** and lots of time.**"** Ha! **M**y whole **summer** is taken up with lessons, camps, trips, and projects. School gets out on a Thursday, and my swimming lessons start on Monday morning. Monday afternoon is when soccer day camp **s**tarts**.** In between, we have this big yard project we all have to help [**to**] with. I think you get the idea. Summer!

Once a **m**onth at school, we do **a** very cool activity called Art Literacy. Parent volunteers come into [**the**] our class and tell us about a certain artist or kind of art**.** They show us slides of the artists**,** their art**,** and even where they lived and worked. **S**ometimes, they have pieces of art to pass around. One of them said, "This will give you a real feel for the art.**"** **T**he best part is the art activity, when we get to create something like the **artist** did, using the same materials, colors, and style. Last month, we learned about Aboriginal [**about**] art from **A**ustralia. It was fun because we got to listen to some **m**usic and heard stories that helped us understand the people and their art**.** I can't wait until next month.

Conventions

Teacher's Guide pages 95, 181–192
Overhead numbers 21–24

Objective

Students will review and apply what they have learned about the trait of conventions.

Reviewing Conventions

Review with students what they have learned about the trait of conventions. Ask students to discuss what conventions are and to explain why they are important in a piece of writing. Then ask them to recall the main points about conventions that are discussed in Unit 6. Students' responses should include the following points:

- Understand the difference between revising and editing.
- Practice identifying errors.
- Use editors' marks correctly.
- Read editor's symbols to edit text.

Applying Conventions

To help students apply what they have learned about the trait of conventions, distribute copies of the Student Rubric for Conventions on page 95 of this Teacher's Guide. Students will use these to score one or more sample papers that can be found beginning on page 116. The papers for conventions are also on overheads 21–24.

Before students score the papers, explain that a rubric is a grading system to determine the score a piece of writing should receive for a particular trait. Preview the Student Rubric for Conventions, pointing out that a paper very strong in conventions receives a score of 6, and a paper very weak in conventions receives a score of 1. Tell students to read the rubric and then to read the paper to be scored. Then tell them to look at the paper and the rubric together to determine the score the paper should receive. Encourage students to make notes on each paper to help them score it. For example, they might use editors' marks to note errors in the paper.

The wrap-up activities in this section are designed for students who have had a chance to work with all six traits of writing. This closure section should not be thought of as a test, but as a reminder, a review, and a chance for students to pull all the traits together.

Wrap-up Activity 1 should take about 15 minutes. Activity 2 has four writing samples, all of which can be completed as a class activity. Allow about 10 minutes for each sample. This will give each student time to read the sample, discuss it with a partner, and determine what the *main* problem is. (There may be more than one problem, but one definitely should stand out.) Allow several minutes for a class discussion.

Wrap-up Activity 1

Traits: In Their Own Words

For use with Student Traitbook pages 106–107

In this activity, the six traits are represented as characters who describe themselves. Each student's task is to see whether he or she can match the name of the trait to the description the character provides. Give students time to read each description, choose a response, and discuss responses with a partner.

Teach this lesson by

- reading each description and choosing a response that correctly matches the description.
- checking answers against the Teacher Rubric.
- making any notes about additional issues during class discussions.

After students have completed their work, have them discuss their responses with a partner. Then discuss the character descriptions with the class. If students do not agree with a response, refer them to specific, relevant lessons or to their student rubrics for more detail on a given trait.

Answers: 1. Conventions, 2. Voice, 3. Organization, 4. Word Choice, 5. Sentence Fluency, 6. Ideas

Making a Diagnosis

For use with Student Traitbook pages 108–111

In order to revise effectively, a writer must be able to read a piece of writing and identify the writing problems. Making such a diagnosis is the first step toward **revision.**

Teach this lesson by

• reading the samples and answering each multiple-choice question.

• checking answers against the rationales that follow each sample.

• making any personal notes about additional issues you wish to raise during class discussions.

After students have made their decisions, discuss the samples with the class. If any students disagree with a diagnosis, let them explain why they disagree. Remember, students should be looking for the main problem—but they also may find additional problems. Make sure that students provide support for each diagnosis they point out.

Response and Rationale for Sample 1

Most students should recognize that the answer is **a, ideas.** This writer jumps quickly from topic to topic. The writer displays a certain amount of voice and plenty of energy, so answer **b** does not apply. The conventions are good, so **d** is not correct. Even if the sentences were reordered, there still would be no main idea, so answer **c** does not apply.

Response and Rationale for Sample 2

The main problem with this text is **c, sentence fluency.** The sentences are all about the same length, and several of them begin the same way. The writing lacks flow and rhythm. Answers **a, b,** and **d** do not apply because the writer has a main idea, the details are organized, and the conventions are correct.

Response and Rationale for Sample 3

The main problem is **b, voice.** The writer seems to have little or no involvement with the topic. The writer reveals no passion, and the word choices are boring and repetitious. The conventions are good, so answer **a** does not apply. The main idea is clear: *I think we should have less homework.* The fluency is rather strong; sentences begin in different ways and are reasonably varied in length, so answer **d** does not apply.

Response and Rationale for Sample 4

The main problem with this sample is **c, organization.** The sudden way in which the writer shifts back and forth from event to event is confusing. The events go from catching a fish to skipping breakfast to looking at the trophy fish on the wall. This paper is fluent, so answer **a** does not apply. It is also rich in detail, so answer **c** does not apply either. The voice is energetic throughout, eliminating answer **d.**

Extensions

- Have students work individually or in pairs to revise one or more of the samples from Wrap-up Activity 2. Read revised papers aloud, and compare them with the originals. Have students revise only ONE of these papers at a time; completing more than one each day may be exhausting for beginning writers. Students need revise only to improve the "problem" trait.

- Ask each student to write a letter that explains why it is important that a piece of writing be strong in the six traits. Work with students to make notes about what to say about the six traits. Students may refer to their notes as they write their letters.

Contents

Sample Papers

Sample Papers: Introduction

The purpose of the Sample Papers is to help students view each trait as a whole. By learning to evaluate a piece of writing, students will become better revisers and writers. This Sample Papers section contains copymasters of Sample Papers. There are four Sample Papers for each trait, twenty-four papers in all. Each Sample Paper is also on an overhead transparency. For each trait, you will find two fairly strong papers and two weaker (in process) papers. The Teacher's Guide will give you suggested scores and a rationale for a particular perspective on every paper.

Using the Sample Papers

You can use each paper alone, in which case you need to allow about 20 minutes (the approximate time required to read, score, and discuss one paper). As an alternative, you can use the papers in pairs, in which case you need to allow at least 40 minutes. You must decide whether your students can focus their attention for such an extended discussion. If you decide to use the papers in pairs, we strongly recommend that you select one strong paper and one weak paper in order to provide contrast.

It is important to present the traits in the order in which they appear in the Student Traitbook and in the Teacher's Guide. You may, however, present the four papers for an individual trait in any order you wish. Read all four papers for the trait at hand in advance, and decide how you will present them. This will also give you time to know the papers well before discussing them with your class.

In advance

- Read the paper aloud *to yourself* so that you know it well and are prepared to share it with students.

At the time of the lesson

- Distribute copies of the appropriate rubric and the Sample Paper. Remind students about key points they should be looking or listening for in response to a particular paper (trait). Keep this list *short*. (Tips for each paper are given in the Teacher's Guide.)

- Read the paper to your students, using as much inflection as the text allows. Some papers have a lot of voice, and some have very little. Be enthusiastic, but don't "invent" voice where it does not exist. (1–2 minutes)

- Have students reflect on the relative strengths or weaknesses of a paper. (4–5 minutes)

- Ask students to commit *in writing* the score a paper should receive for a given trait. Do not share your own opinion yet. (1 minute)

- If you use hard copies of the papers, students may be asked to perform simple tasks, such as underlining favorite words or circling overused words. Allow time for this activity before discussing each paper. (1–2 minutes)

- Ask students to compare responses with a partner. Have them answer a question such as *Why do you think this paper is strong in ideas?* (3–4 minutes)

- When partners have finished talking, discuss the paper with the class as a whole. Ask how many students considered the paper strong and how many considered it weak. Record the numbers and compare them. (2 minutes)

- Lead a full-class discussion. Ask students to justify their decisions: Why did they think the paper was strong or weak? Suggested questions for each paper are provided in the Teacher's Guide. (5 minutes or less)

Sample Papers

IDEAS

Paper 1: Cafeteria (Score: 2)*

Paper 2: My Cookie Surprise (Score: 6)

Paper 3: The Deer Family (Score: 3)

Paper 4: My Most Embarrassing Moment (Score: 5)

ORGANIZATION

Paper 5: Egypt (Score: 6)

Paper 6: The Embarrassing Play (Score: 3)

Paper 7: How to Give a Haircut (Score: 6)

Paper 8: A New Car (Score: 2)

VOICE

Paper 9: Accidental Haircut (Score: 5)

Paper 10: Cats Make the Best Pets (Score: 3)

Paper 11: Homework Is Important (Score: 2)

Paper 12: My Brother the Pain (Score: 6)

WORD CHOICE

Paper 13: Engine (Score: 4)

Paper 14: King of the Surf (Score: 6)

Paper 15: Movies Are My Favorite Thing (Score: 2)

Paper 16: Life on the Prairie (Score: 2)

SENTENCE FLUENCY

Paper 17: Alligator (Score: 2)

Paper 18: Chinese Dragon (Score: 5)

Paper 19: Flying (Score: 6)

Paper 20: Shopping (Score: 3)

CONVENTIONS

Paper 21: Flank Steak and Other Treats (Score: 6)

Paper 22: A Career in Nursing (Score: 2)

Paper 23: The Best Hideout (Score: 4)

Paper 24: Pizza Mania (Score: 2)

*See the appendix for scores on a 5-point rubric.

Sample Paper 1: Cafeteria

Objective

Students will learn that details add interest to writing and help clarify *ideas.*

Materials

Student Rubric for Ideas (Teacher's Guide page 5)

Sample Paper 1: Cafeteria (Teacher's Guide page 122 and/or Overhead 1)

Scoring the Paper

1. Distribute copies of the sample paper and the Student Rubric for Ideas. Use the rubric to focus students' attention on the key features of the trait of IDEAS—main idea and details. Review that a detail is important or interesting information.

2. Have students think about these questions as they listen to you read the paper: *Does the writer stay focused on the main topic (the cafeteria)? Does the writer provide enough information to help readers picture students during their lunch break?*

3. Ask students to score the paper *individually,* using the rubric. They should mark their scores in writing, putting an **X** in the appropriate blank. (If students do not have copies of the sample paper, they can write on separate sheets of paper.)

4. Ask students to compare their responses with those of a partner. They should take a few minutes to talk about the paper and ask each other questions. Expect this process to be slow at first; they will talk more and come to agreement faster as time goes on.

5. After three or four minutes, ask students to write their reasons for scoring the paper as they did.

Discussing the Paper

Discuss the paper with the class. Ask students to say what scores they gave the paper and why. The *why* is the most important part in deepening their understanding. Use the following questions to encourage discussion:

• What is the main idea? Is it easy to identify?

• Do the details suggest that this writer has taken a close look at the lunch scene? Can you picture the students at the lunch table?

• Are the details things most of us would know?

• What questions do you still have?

*Rationale for the Score**

Most students should see this paper as **weak.** It received a score of **2** on the 6-point rubric. It has a main idea: *The cafeteria is chaotic during the lunch hour.* The writer does include some details: the students mixing ketchup and milk or talking with their mouths full. These descriptions create images in the reader's mind. The problem is that we do not have enough information for a complete picture. More detail would help. In addition, the writer needs to include more sensory information, such as sounds, smells, and tastes.

Extensions

1. Ask each student to look at a piece of his or her own writing. Is the main idea clear? If not, what can be done to make it clear? Are the details interesting? Will additions or changes help?

2. Start with a general statement: *The room was messy.* Ask students to suggest details to flesh out the picture and make the description vivid. Tell students not to use the word *messy.*

3. Ask student pairs to revise "Cafeteria," adding details to make it more descriptive. Then ask volunteers to read aloud their before and after versions.

*See Teacher's Guide page 195 for a 5-point rubric and page 207 for the score.

Sample Paper 1: IDEAS

Cafeteria

Kids in our cafeteria are very loud and also yell a lot. They all talk with their mouths full of food. Some boys make gross mixtures with milk and ketchup. Things are spilling on the floor everywhere. Some people do rude stuff. Fortunately, lunch is only 20 minutes long. Any more time in the cafeteria would make me sick.

Mark the score that this paper should receive in the trait of IDEAS. Read your rubric for Ideas to help you decide. Then write your reason for the score.

___ 1 ___ 2 ___ 3 ___ 4 ___ 5 ___ 6

_____

_____

Compare your score with your partner's. How did you do?

___ We matched **exactly!**

___ We matched within **one point**—pretty good!

___ We were **two points or more** apart. We need to discuss this.

Sample Paper 2: My Cookie Surprise

Objective

Students will understand how important relevant details are in a piece of writing.

Materials

Student Rubric for Ideas (Teacher's Guide page 5)

Sample Paper 2: My Cookie Surprise (Teacher's Guide page 125 and/or Overhead 2)

Scoring the Paper

1. Distribute copies of the sample paper and the Student Rubric for Ideas. Use the rubric to focus students' attention on the key features of the trait of IDEAS—main idea and details. The paper should be clear and easy to understand.

2. Have students think about these questions as they listen to you read the paper: *Is the main idea clear and easy to understand? Why or why not?*

3. Ask students to score the paper *individually,* using the rubric. They should mark their scores in writing, putting an **X** in the appropriate blank. (If students do not have copies of the sample paper, they can write on separate sheets of paper.)

4. Ask students to compare their responses with those of a partner. They should take a few minutes to talk about the paper and ask each other questions. Expect this process to be slow at first; they will talk more and come to agreement faster as time goes on.

Discussing the Paper

Discuss the paper with the class. Ask students to say what scores they gave the paper and why. The *why* is the most important part in deepening their understanding. Use the following questions to encourage discussion:

• Can you picture what is happening in this paper?

• What is the writer's main idea? Is it easy to identify?

• What ideas can you picture most clearly?

• Do the details in the paper relate to the main idea?

Rationale for the Score*

Most students should see this paper as **strong.** It received a score of **6** on the 6-point rubric. The writer paints a clear, vivid picture of an unusual experience, and the images of biting into the "hard" cookie and using a wad of paper to stop the bleeding are easy to visualize. The writer uses personal experience and excellent recall of the situation to make the story lively and interesting.

Extensions

1. Ask each student to look at a piece of his or her own writing. Is the main idea clear? If not, what can be done to make it clear? Are the details interesting? Will additions or changes help?

2. Ask each student to write a story about losing a tooth. Point out that details might include how loose the tooth was; whether it was a front tooth, a molar, or some other tooth; and how the tooth finally came out.

*See Teacher's Guide page 195 for a 5-point rubric and page 207 for the score.

Sample Paper 2: IDEAS

My Cookie Surprise

Munch, munch. That's what I was doing when it happened. I was eight years old and on a trip to Michigan to see my cousins when I got my unexpected dessert.

I was eating my dinner on the airplane. I ripped off the plastic around my granola cookie. Then I bit into it and WOW! That was one hard cookie!

I took the cookie out of my mouth, and what did I see? A tooth was stuck in the cookie! I unbuckled my seat belt, walked down the aisle as quickly as I could, and locked myself in the tiny bathroom.

When I looked in the mirror, I saw a blank space in my bottom row of teeth. I got a paper towel to stop the blood. I stuffed it in so that blood would not drip out and stain my clothes. I could barely close my mouth around that big wad of paper. I walked back to my seat slowly, hoping that no one would notice the wad of paper puffing out my lips and cheeks. I know I must have looked like an overgrown chipmunk.

I'll give you some important advice. If you have a loose tooth, don't crunch down on an airplane cookie!

Mark the score that this paper should receive in the trait of IDEAS.
Read your rubric for Ideas to help you decide.

___1 ___2 ___3 ___4 ___5 ___6

Sample Paper 3: The Deer Family

Objective

Students will learn the importance of supplying a sufficient number of relevant details to support and clarify a main idea.

Materials

Student Rubric for Ideas (Teacher's Guide page 5)

Sample Paper 3: The Deer Family (Teacher's Guide page 128 and/or Overhead 3)

Scoring the Paper

1. Distribute copies of the sample paper and the Student Rubric for Ideas. Use the rubric to focus students' attention on the key features of the trait of IDEAS—main idea and details. Students should ask themselves whether the details are sufficient to answer a reader's questions about deer.

2. Have students think about these questions as they listen to you read the paper: *Are there enough details to help you understand about deer? Are there details that do not support the main idea?*

3. Ask students to score the paper *individually,* using the rubric. They should mark their scores in writing, putting an **X** in the appropriate blank. (If students do not have copies of the sample paper, they can write on separate sheets of paper.)

4. Ask students to compare their responses with those of a partner. They should take a few minutes to talk about the paper and ask each other questions. Expect this process to be slow at first; they will talk more and come to agreement faster as time goes on.

5. After three or four minutes, ask students to write their reasons for scoring the paper as they did.

Discussing the Paper

Discuss the paper with the class. Ask students to say what scores they gave the paper and why. The *why* is the most important part in deepening their understanding. Use the following questions to encourage discussion:

• What is the writer's main idea? Is it easy to identify?

• Does the writer choose good details to help make the main idea clear?

• Are you left with any questions about deer? If so, what are they?

• Is there any filler (unneeded information) in the paper?

*Rationale for the Score**

Most students should see this paper as **weak.** It received a score of **3** on the 6-point rubric because much more information is needed to make this paper complete. The main idea could be that a deer's life span is short because its life is hard. The main idea also might be that the deer is a successful animal species because it has adapted to various conditions throughout the world. The writer makes both points but does not offer enough support for either of them.

Extensions

1. Ask each student to look at a piece of his or her own writing. Is the main idea clear? If not, what can be done to make it clear? Are there enough details to support the main idea? If not, what ideas could be added or expanded?

2. Have students research to find three interesting facts about deer. Then have students use the information to write short paragraphs about deer. Have them compare their work to this author's work.

*See Teacher's Guide page 195 for a 5-point rubric and page 207 for the score.

Sample Paper 3: IDEAS

The Deer Family

The deer family is one of the most successful families of large mammals in the world. Deer originally were found only in Asia, but they have spread all around the world and live in different types of habitats. Caribou, moose, and elk are among the types of deer. Even though they have spread around the world, life isn't easy for deer. They usually live for only five years.

Mark the score that this paper should receive in the trait of IDEAS. Read your rubric for Ideas to help you decide. Then write your reason for the score.

___ 1 ___ 2 ___ 3 ___ 4 ___ 5 ___ 6

_____

_____

Compare your score with your partner's. How did you do?

___ We matched **exactly!**

___ We matched within **one point**—pretty good!

___ We were **two points or more** apart. We need to discuss this.

Sample Paper 4: My Most Embarrassing Moment

Objective

Students will understand that one brief, well-described moment can be the basis for a full description or story.

Materials

Student Rubric for Ideas (Teacher's Guide page 5)
Sample Paper 4: My Most Embarrassing Moment (Teacher's Guide page 131 and/or Overhead 4)

Scoring the Paper

1. Distribute copies of the sample paper and the Student Rubric for Ideas. Use the rubric to focus students' attention on the key features of the trait of IDEAS—main idea and details. Students should also check for filler—unnecessary information.

2. Have students think about these questions as they listen to you read the paper: *Are there enough details to help you understand the paper? Are there extra details here to support the main idea?*

3. Ask students to score the paper *individually,* using the rubric. They should mark their scores in writing, putting an **X** in the appropriate blank. (If students do not have copies of the sample paper, they can write on separate sheets of paper.)

4. Ask students to compare their responses with those of a partner. They should take a few minutes to talk about the paper and ask each other questions. Expect this process to be slow at first; they will talk more and come to agreement faster as time goes on.

Discussing the Paper

Discuss the paper with the class. Ask students to say what scores they gave the paper and why. The *why* is the most important part in deepening their understanding. Use the following questions to encourage discussion:

- Does this story have a main idea? If so, what is it?
- Does this writer provide a clear picture of an embarrassing moment?
- Are you left with questions, or does the writer provide enough information?
- Is there anything you would like to know more about?
- Is any information unnecessary? If so, what ideas could be omitted?

*Rationale for the Score**

Most students should see this paper as **strong.** It received a score of **5** on the 6-point rubric because it provides a complete story and makes a clear point: *Take time to know what you are doing if you want to avoid embarrassing situations!* More sensory detail and some dialogue would have improved the story.

Extensions

1. Ask each student to look at a piece of his or her own writing. Is the main idea clear? Are the details well chosen? Could sensory detail or dialogue add important or interesting information?

2. Work with students to brainstorm a list of embarrassing moments. (Be sure to let students know that they need not share information that they prefer to keep private.) Then ask students to choose one moment and write a brief paragraph about what happened. When they are finished, have them underline details they think bring the topic to life. Volunteers can share their paragraphs.

3. Share your own embarrassing moment story. Have some fun by telling it orally first. Give students the main idea, and then let them ask questions that bring out the details. Fill out your draft by responding to their questions.

4. As an alternative, create a series of "travel" adventures. Travel can include anything from a cross-country trip to a bicycle or bus ride. Try to focus on one moment from the travel experience: one adventure or one impression. Encourage students NOT to write a saga about the entire trip.

*See Teacher's Guide page 195 for a 5-point rubric and page 208 for the score.

name: .... date: ....

Sample Paper 4: IDEAS

My Most Embarrassing Moment

My most embarrassing moment happened at an airport when my family and I were taking a trip. I had too much soda to drink on the plane, and my mom kept trying to get me to go to the bathroom. I just didn't want to because airplane bathrooms are so cramped. So I didn't go. By the time the plane landed, I felt like a giant water balloon about to explode. Naturally, I ran for the restroom the first chance I got. I didn't even stop to look at the sign on the door. I was just following my cousin Brad. Yikes! I walked right in on a whole bunch of boys. I do not know how many there were, but it seemed like about a hundred, and they were all staring at me! I felt my face going red. I ran out as fast as I could and into the girls' bathroom. I could not wait to close the door behind me! I stayed in there a really long time, hoping all the boys would be gone when I came out. We almost missed our connecting flight because I waited so long. My mom was laughing as though it were the funniest thing that ever happened in the whole world. From that day to this, I have always looked at the sign on the door, no matter how desperate I might be.

Mark the score that this paper should receive in the trait of IDEAS.
Read your rubric for Ideas to help you decide.

____ 1 ____ 2 ____ 3 ____ 4 ____ 5 ____ 6

Organization

Sample Paper 5: Egypt

Objective

Students will understand the importance of an orderly presentation of ideas, strong transitions, and a good lead and conclusion.

Materials

Student Rubric for Organization (Teacher's Guide page 23)

Sample Paper 5: Egypt (Teacher's Guide page 134 and/or Overhead 5)

Scoring the Paper

1. Distribute copies of the sample paper and the Student Rubric for Organization. Use the rubric to focus students' attention on the key features of the trait of ORGANIZATION. In particular, students should ask themselves whether the paper is easy to follow and whether it has a strong lead and an effective conclusion.

2. Have students think about these questions as they listen to you read the paper: *Can you follow what the writer is saying? Has the writer used a pattern that makes sense?*

3. Ask students to score the paper *individually,* using the rubric. They should mark their scores in writing, putting an **X** in the appropriate blank. (If students do not have copies of the sample paper, they can write on separate sheets of paper.)

4. Ask students to compare their responses with those of a partner. They should take a few minutes to talk about the paper and ask each other questions. Expect this process to be slow at first; they will talk more and come to agreement faster as time goes on.

5. After three or four minutes, ask students to write their reasons for scoring the paper as they did.

Discussing the Paper

Discuss the paper with the class. Ask students to say what scores they gave the paper and why. The *why* is the most important part in deepening their understanding. Use the following questions to encourage discussion:

- Do you like the lead for this paper? Why?

- Do you like the the conclusion? Why?

- Is the paper easy to follow? Do you ever feel confused?

- Does the writer ever wander from the main topic? If so, where does this happen?

*Rationale for the Score**

Most students should see this paper as **strong.** It received a score of **6** on the 6-point rubric because it is easy to follow and moves smoothly from point to point. The lead is striking: *There is more to Egypt than mummies and pyramids.* The ending also works well: *Think of a land where having the first and the biggest is not that unusual.* The information presented is well organized and the writer connects each point to the main idea without wandering off topic.

Extensions

1. Ask each student to look at a piece of his or her own writing. Are the key points and details in order? If not, suggest that the students re-organize the material. Does the piece have a strong lead? If not, the student can write a new one. Does it have a strong conclusion? If not, the student can revise for a more effective ending.

2. Think of other ways the writer could have started this paper. As a class, write two or three other leads that would also work well. Have students suggest ideas for conclusions, too.

3. Have the class score "Egypt" for the trait of IDEAS. Discuss the students' scores and the reasons for their scores.

*See Teacher's Guide page 196 for a 5-point rubric and page 208 for the score.

Sample Paper 5: ORGANIZATION

Egypt

There is more to Egypt than mummies and pyramids. For starters, the Nile River is in Egypt. The Nile is the longest river in the world. Without it, the Egyptians would be in big trouble because it is a major source of water for many people. Part of the world's biggest desert, the Sahara, is also in Egypt. It covers over half of Egypt, in fact, about 97 percent of the country! Another interesting fact about Egypt is that paper was invented there. Egyptians made paper from a plant, papyrus, which grows close to the Nile. So when you think of Egypt, don't just picture the pyramids in your head. Think of a land where having the first and the biggest is not that unusual.

Mark the score that this paper should receive in the trait of ORGANIZATION. Read your rubric for Organization to help you decide. Then write your reason for the score.

___ 1 ___ 2 ___ 3 ___ 4 ___ 5 ___ 6

_____

_____

Compare your score with your partner's. How did you do?

____ We matched **exactly!**

____ We matched within **one point**—pretty good!

____ We were **two points or more** apart. We need to discuss this.

Sample Paper 6: The Embarrassing Play

Objective

Students will recognize that when a writer strays from the topic, a paper is hard to follow.

Materials

Student Rubric for Organization (Teacher's Guide page 23)

Sample Paper 6: The Embarrassing Play (Teacher's Guide page 137 and/or Overhead 6)

Scoring the Paper

1. Distribute copies of the sample paper and the Student Rubric for Organization. Use the rubric to focus students' attention on the key features of the trait of ORGANIZATION. In particular, students should ask themselves whether the paper is easy to follow and whether it has a strong lead and an effective conclusion.

2. Have students think about these questions as they listen to you read the paper: *Does the writer stick to the main point? Is all the information organized in a logical pattern?*

3. Ask students to score the paper *individually*, using the rubric. They should mark their scores in writing, putting an **X** in the appropriate blank. (If students do not have copies of the sample paper, they can write on separate sheets of paper.)

4. Ask students to compare their responses with those of a partner. They should take a few minutes to talk about the paper and ask each other questions. Expect this process to be slow at first; they will talk more and come to agreement faster as time goes on.

5. After three or four minutes, ask students to write their reasons for scoring the paper as they did.

Discussing the Paper

Discuss the paper with the class. Ask students to say what scores they gave the paper and why. The *why* is the most important part in deepening their understanding. Use the following questions to encourage discussion:

• Do you like this paper's lead? Why?

• Do you like this paper's conclusion? Why?

• Is the paper easy to follow? Does the writer ever wander from the main topic or point? If so, where?

Rationale for the Score*

Most students should see this paper as somewhat **weak.** It received a score of **3** on the 6-point rubric because the writer wanders enough from the main idea to confuse the reader. The story begins with the embarrassment of having the little sister go on the stage—but before this can be developed at all, the writer introduces a discussion of fashion. The writer returns to the embarrassing moment in the end, but the reader cannot be sure which moment he or she is referring to. The lead shows promise, but the writer does not follow up. The conclusion is ambiguous.

Extensions

1. Ask each student to look at a piece of his or her own writing. Does the lead set the stage for what follows—or does the writer stray from the topic? Does the conclusion follow from the rest of the paper, or is it simply tacked on to bring the piece to an end? Have students revise as necessary.

2. Have students rewrite "The Embarrassing Play" from the little sister's point of view or from the director's point of view. How does this change affect the organization? Does it change the main idea as well?

*See Teacher's Guide page 196 for a 5-point rubric and page 208 for the score.

Sample Paper 6: ORGANIZATION

The Embarrassing Play

My most embarrassing moment happened last year when my little sister ran on stage in the middle of my school play.

I was embarrassed at the dance recital when I had to wear a ridiculous ugly yellow raincoat and a hat that a 3-year-old would wear. I was 8 at the time and liked clothes that didn't make me look like a little kid. The dance teacher had chosen my outfit and thought I looked cute. I wanted to quit and not perform at all, but I was brave and did it anyway. I will never forget this embarrassing moment.

Mark the score that this paper should receive in the trait of ORGANIZATION. Read your rubric for Organization to help you decide. Then write your reason for the score.

___ 1 ___ 2 ___ 3 ___ 4 ___ 5 ___ 6

_____

_____

Compare your score with your partner's. How did you do?

____ We matched **exactly!**

____ We matched within **one point**—pretty good!

____ We were **two points or more** apart. We need to discuss this.

Sample Paper 7: How to Give a Haircut

Objective

Students will understand the importance of arranging details in a logical order.

Materials

Student Rubric for Organization (Teacher's Guide page 23)

Sample Paper 7: How to Give a Haircut (Teacher's Guide page 140 and/or Overhead 7)

Scoring the Paper

1. Distribute copies of the sample paper and the Student Rubric for Organization. Use the rubric to focus students' attention on the key features of the trait of ORGANIZATION. In particular, students should ask themselves whether the paper is easy to follow, whether it wanders from point to point, and whether it has a strong lead and an effective conclusion.

2. Have students think about these questions as they listen to you read the paper: *Is this paper easy to follow? Are the lead and the conclusion strong?*

3. Ask students to score the paper *individually,* using the rubric. They should mark their scores in writing, putting an **X** in the appropriate blank. (If students do not have copies of the sample paper, they can write on separate sheets of paper.)

4. Ask students to compare their responses with those of a partner. They should take a few minutes to talk about the paper and ask each other questions. Expect this process to be slow at first; they will talk more and come to agreement faster as time goes on.

Discussing the Paper

Discuss the paper with the class. Ask students to say what scores they gave the paper and why. The *why* is the most important part in deepening their understanding. Use the following questions to encourage discussion:

- Is this paper easy to follow? Are the instructions in a clear, logical order? Explain.
- Do you like the lead? Why or why not?
- Do you like the conclusion? Why or why not?
- Would you do anything differently to strengthen this paper's organization?

*Rationale for the Score**

Most students should see this paper as very **strong.** It received a score of **6** on the 6-point rubric because it is easy to follow, and the writer does not wander from the main topic. The writer includes a step-by-step pattern, though it is also divided into two major sections: what the reader will need for the project and how to do it. In this way, the paper is set up like a recipe. The lead and the conclusion are strong. The writer starts by explaining that it is not necessary to spend a fortune to get a good haircut—a friend could do it! That's an intriguing introduction, and it sets the paper up well. The conclusion is humorous and effective.

Extensions

1. Ask each student to write a how-to paper that follows the same organizational structure as "How to Give a Haircut." After they write, have volunteers share papers and talk about how easy it is to follow this pattern.

2. Ask each student to look at a piece of his or her own writing to identify its organizational pattern. (Possibilities: Step-by-step, comparison-contrast, chronological order, most important to least important, answers to readers' main questions, argument and counterargument, reasons to adopt a viewpoint or take action, and so on.)

3. Ask each student to write two other conclusions for "How to Give a Haircut." Can anyone improve on the author's conclusion?

*See Teacher's Guide page 196 for a 5-point rubric and page 209 for the score.

Sample Paper 7: ORGANIZATION

How to Give a Haircut

You probably think you need to spend tons of money to get a good haircut, but that's not true. You can learn to cut a friend's hair. Here's all you need: a big sheet or tarp to catch the falling hair (very important!), a misting spray bottle to wet your friend's hair, a waterproof cape to put over your friend's shoulders, a comb to untangle the hair, and barber scissors you can buy at any drugstore. Also, make sure your mom or dad is there to help you.

Now comes the fun part. First, fasten the waterproof cape around your friend's neck. Next, wet your friend's hair because dry hair is hard to cut. Using the comb, part the hair right down the middle. Then, start parting again from one side or the other. Pull one section out straight between your fingers, and cut the ends of the section neatly. Cut about a half inch at a time. You can always cut more, but you can't glue it back on! Repeat this process until you have finished the haircut. When you are done, blow dry the hair, and let your friend look in the mirror—unless, of course, you have made a mistake. In that case, pretend you can't find your mirror, and gently remind your friend that this haircut was free.

Mark the score that this paper should receive in the trait of ORGANIZATION. Read your rubric for Organization to help you decide.

___ 1 ___ 2 ___ 3 ___ 4 ___ 5 ___ 6

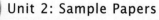

Sample Paper 8: A New Car

Objective

Students will recognize the importance of presenting events in a logical order and of relating the lead and the conclusion to the rest of the paper.

Materials

Student Rubric for Organization (Teacher's Guide page 23)

Sample Paper 8: A New Car (Teacher's Guide page 143 and/or Overhead 8)

Scoring the Paper

1. Distribute copies of the sample paper and the Student Rubric for Organization. Use the rubric to focus students' attention on the key features of the trait of ORGANIZATION. In particular, students should ask themselves whether the paper is easy to follow, whether it has any identifiable organizational pattern, and whether it has a strong lead and an effective conclusion.

2. Have students think about these questions as they listen to you read the paper: *Is this paper easy to follow? Is the order of information logical?*

3. Ask students to score the paper *individually,* using the rubric. They should mark their scores in writing, putting an **X** in the appropriate blank. (If students do not have copies of the sample paper, they can write on separate sheets of paper.)

4. Ask students to compare their responses with those of a partner. They should take a few minutes to talk about the paper and ask each other questions. Expect this process to be slow at first; they will talk more and come to agreement faster as time goes on.

5. After three or four minutes, ask students to write their reasons for scoring the paper as they did.

Discussing the Paper

Discuss the paper with the class. Ask students to say what scores they gave the paper and why. The *why* is the most important part in deepening their understanding. Use the following questions to encourage discussion:

- Do you like the lead? Why? Does the rest of the paper follow logically from the lead?

- Do you see any pattern in the organizational structure? If so, can you describe it?

- Do you like the conclusion? Why or why not?

- What would you do to strengthen this paper's organization?

*Rationale for the Score**

Though it has a lot of voice and is fun to read, most students should see this paper as somewhat **weak.** It received a score of **2** on the 6-point rubric because it wanders and does not connect key points to any main idea. The story goes from the new family car to the difficulties of coping with a little brother to the challenges of living with a less than brilliant dog to next year's school—and finally back to the car. The lead is rather weak: *Last night my parents bought a new car.* The ending is better: *Oh well, parents are good at some things—like picking out new cars!* Still, neither connects to the writer's main points. This writer really has not settled on any one topic, and that's one reason for the weak organization.

Extensions

1. Have students brainstorm possible main topics for this paper. Have them decide what one topic can be found from all the scattered ideas that the writer lists. Which topic do they think would make the strongest paper?

2. Choose one of the topics from the brainstormed list, and ask students to write two leads for that topic. Ask volunteers to read their leads aloud and talk about how this topic might have allowed the writer more freedom of expression.

3. Have each student draft a short note to the writer, offering some advice for using better organization.

*See Teacher's Guide page 196 for a 5-point rubric and page 209 for the score.

Sample Paper 8: ORGANIZATION

A New Car

Last night my parents bought a new car. It is blue. We went for a ride in it. I had to sit in the back seat with my little brother. He is a total nuisance! Every five minutes he wanted to stop for something to eat. He has this whiny, shrill voice that just about blows your eardrums out. It actually hurts. If I complain about him, my mother says, "Don't be mean. He's just five." Why do parents always take the little kid's side? When I am playing with the dog, my brother will tease him. I can't get Ringo to do anything, and then I am the one who gets blamed for making the dog angry. It's too much for me. I am not sure dogs even have moods. They're not that smart. At least our dog isn't. He doesn't even notice when you put his food out for him—even if you put it right in the middle of the room! One good thing is that I am almost in sixth grade, so I am going to a different school next year. I am going to play basketball, and I can't wait! The car is OK. I told my dad he made a good choice, except that he should have gotten the CD player. Oh well, parents are good at some things—like picking out new cars!

Mark the score that this paper should receive in the trait of ORGANIZATION. Read your rubric for Organization to help you decide. Then write your reason for the score.

___ 1 ___ 2 ___ 3 ___ 4 ___ 5 ___ 6

_____

_____

Unit 3 Voice

Sample Paper 9: Accidental Haircut

Objective

Students will understand that interest and enthusiasm allow voice to come through.

Materials

Student Rubric for Voice (Teacher's Guide page 41)

Sample Paper 9: Accidental Haircut (Teacher's Guide page 146 and/or Overhead 9)

Scoring the Paper

1. Distribute copies of the sample paper and the Student Rubric for Voice. Use the rubric to focus students' attention on the key features of the trait of VOICE. In particular, students should look and listen for energy, appeal, some sign of emotion or individuality—a paper that truly stands out from others.

2. Have students think about these questions as they listen to you read the paper: *Does this writer's voice come through? Does it have energy?*

3. Ask students to score the paper *individually,* using the rubric. They should mark their scores in writing, putting an **X** in the appropriate blank. (If students do not have copies of the sample paper, they can write on separate sheets of paper.)

4. Ask students to compare their responses with those of a partner. They should take a few minutes to talk about the paper and ask each other questions. Expect this process to be slow at first; they will talk more and come to agreement faster as time goes on.

5. After three or four minutes, ask students to write their reasons for scoring the paper as they did.

Discussing the Paper

Discuss the paper with the class. Ask students to say what scores they gave the paper and why. The *why* is the most important part in deepening their understanding. Use the following questions to encourage discussion:

• Did you enjoy this story? Did you want to hear more? Why?

• Would you read this aloud to a friend? Why or why not?

• Does this writer seem to enjoy telling this story? What clues do we have about how the writer feels?

• Can you point to a place in the paper where the voice is strongest?

*Rationale for the Score**

Most students should see this paper as **strong.** It received a score of **5** on the 6-point rubric. The writer creates vivid impressions—her horror at having the curly comb caught in her hair, her worry that her mother will discover her problem (which she does), and her frenzy over having her hair cut—not to mention the semi-disastrous results. The writer's personality comes through clearly. This is definitely a read-aloud paper.

Extensions

1. Ask students to identify those moments in "Accidental Haircut" where the voice is strongest. Would they revise any part of this paper? If so, take time to try some revisions.

2. Ask students to gather in small groups and read samples of their own writing aloud. They should listen for moments of voice in one another's writing and comment on those parts they think are strongest. Participate as a writer/reader in one of the groups.

3. Have each student write a paragraph about a personal experience—good or bad. Have volunteers share their paragraphs with the class.

*See Teacher's Guide page 197 for a 5-point rubric and page 209 for the score.

Sample Paper 9: VOICE

Accidental Haircut

I will never forget my "accidental" haircut. I was just combing my hair in the bathroom one day. I was using my mom's curly comb when the comb got stuck in my hair! I pulled and pulled and finally got it out. When I looked in the mirror, though, I saw a huge knot.

My mom came in while I was trying to hide my knot, but it was too late. She saw it. "Please, no scissors; please, no scissors!" I kept saying, but it was no use. She already had the scissors in her hand! What had I gotten myself into? She started snipping and clipping, tugging and pulling—and then . . . she was done.

I went to look in the mirror, and I almost flipped! Most of my hair was gone! Mom had cut out the knot and then cut the hair on the other side to make it even. "How am I supposed to go around like this?" I asked her. She had no sympathy. "Put on a hat, or think about it as a new hair style," she said. She acted as though people got their hair cut like this every day.

Mark the score that this paper should receive in the trait of VOICE. Read your rubric for Voice to help you decide. Then write your reason for the score.

____ 1 ____ 2 ____ 3 ____ 4 ____ 5 ____ 6

_____

_____

Sample Paper 10: Cats Make the Best Pets

Objective

Students will know that when a writer likes a topic and speaks honestly about it, the voice is strong.

Materials

Student Rubric for Voice (Teacher's Guide page 41)

Sample Paper 10: Cats Make the Best Pets (Teacher's Guide page 149 and/or Overhead 10)

Scoring the Paper

1. Distribute copies of the sample paper and the Student Rubric for Voice. Use the rubric to focus students' attention on the key features of the trait of VOICE. In particular, students should look and listen for energy, appeal, some sign of emotion or individuality—a paper that truly stands out from others.

2. Have students think about these questions as they listen to you read the paper: *Is this paper enjoyable to listen to or read? Why or why not?*

3. Ask students to score the paper *individually,* using the rubric. They should mark their scores in writing, putting an **X** in the appropriate blank. (If students do not have copies of the sample paper, they can write on separate sheets of paper.)

4. Ask students to compare their responses with those of a partner. They should take a few minutes to talk about the paper and ask each other questions. Expect this process to be slow at first; they will talk more and come to agreement faster as time goes on.

5. After three or four minutes, ask students to write their reasons for scoring the paper as they did.

Discussing the Paper

Discuss the paper with the class. Ask students to say what scores they gave the paper and why. The *why* is the most important part in deepening their understanding. Use the following questions to encourage discussion:

- Can you tell how the writer feels about cats? Explain.
- Are some moments stronger than others? If so, where do these strong moments occur?
- Would you read this aloud to a friend? Why or why not?
- Does this writer seem to enjoy writing about cats?
- If you read another piece of writing by the same author, do you think you would recognize the voice? Why or why not?

Rationale for the Score*

Most students should see this paper as somewhat **weak.** It received a score of **3** on the 6-point rubric because it is not consistently energetic, even though it has moments of strong voice. The writer seems to genuinely love cats and appreciates the fact that they are independent and easy to care for. This is not a high-energy paper, however. The voice is more sincere and functional than passionate or distinctive.

Extensions

1. Have each student work with a partner. Ask partners to revise "Cats Make the Best Pets" for the trait of VOICE. They may add, delete, or change any details they wish. Ask them first to imagine all the things that make cats great pets (and perhaps a few drawbacks, as well). They should then revise the paper so that strong voice comes through. Read revisions aloud.

2. Suggest that each student review any piece of writing on which he or she is currently working to identify places where the voice needs improvement. Have students mark these passages. Then have students revise the paper for stronger voice.

*See Teacher's Guide page 197 for a 5-point rubric and page 210 for the score.

Sample Paper 10: VOICE

Cats Make the Best Pets

A cat is the best house pet a family can have. Cats are soft and cuddly and like to sit indoors with people. You can leave them for a day or two, and they are happy to go out the cat door and come back when they are ready. They meow a little, but they don't really make much noise. They don't eat much, so they are not very expensive to keep. They can also have cute kittens, which are fun to have around.

Mark the score that this paper should receive in the trait of VOICE. Read your rubric for Voice to help you decide. Then write your reason for the score.

___ 1 ___ 2 ___ 3 ___ 4 ___ 5 ___ 6

_____

_____

Compare your score with your partner's. How did you do?

___ We matched **exactly!**

___ We matched within **one point**—pretty good!

___ We were **two points or more** apart. We need to discuss this.

Sample Paper 11: Homework Is Important

Objective

Students will understand that a writer's lack of interest in a topic will result in a paper with little or no voice.

Materials

Student Rubric for Voice (Teacher's Guide page 41)

Sample Paper 11: Homework Is Important (Teacher's Guide page 152 and/or Overhead 11)

Scoring the Paper

1. Distribute copies of the sample paper and the Student Rubric for Voice. Use the rubric to focus students' attention on the key features of the trait of VOICE. In particular, students should look and listen for energy, liveliness, or individuality—a paper that truly stands out from others.

2. Have students think about these questions as they listen to you read the paper: *Is this paper enjoyable to listen to or read? Do you think the writer enjoyed writing the paper?*

3. Ask students to score the paper *individually*, using the rubric. They should mark their scores in writing, putting an **X** in the appropriate blank. (If students do not have copies of the sample paper, they can write on separate sheets of paper.)

4. Ask students to compare their responses with those of a partner. They should take a few minutes to talk about the paper and ask each other questions. Expect this process to be slow at first; they will talk more and come to agreement faster as time goes on.

5. After three or four minutes, ask students to write their reasons for scoring the paper as they did.

Discussing the Paper

Discuss the paper with the class. Ask students to say what scores they gave the paper and why. The *why* is the most important part in deepening their understanding. Use the following questions to encourage discussion:

• Do you think you might recognize this writer's voice in another piece of writing? Why?

• Could you identify any moments of strong voice?

• How would you describe this writer's voice?

• What specific steps would you take to revise this piece for voice?

• Do you think the writer is interested in this topic? What clues tell you how the writer feels?

*Rationale for the Score**

Most students should see this paper as **weak.** It has very little energy, and its repetition of key words and ideas is flat and boring. It received a score of **2** on the 6-point rubric. The writer does not appear particularly engaged and certainly is writing about a topic that holds little interest for him or her. The generalities that fill the paper—homework is important, homework makes you smart, smart people are interesting—are commonly held beliefs that readers have heard before.

Extensions

1. Have the class brainstorm some thoughts about homework—positive or negative. Have students use this list of thoughts to draft paragraphs about their attitude toward homework. They should tell what they like and dislike about homework, making sure they say it with strong voice.

2. Ask each student to analyze voice in a piece of his or her own writing. Have students identify any passages that are strong in voice and any passages that need a voice revision. Then tell students to revise those passages that are weak in voice.

*See Teacher's Guide page 197 for a 5-point rubric and page 210 for the score.

Sample Paper 11: VOICE

Homework Is Important

Doing your homework helps you in many ways. If you didn't have homework you would never understand or get smarter at anything. But if you do your homework, you'll find that life is easier.

You need to know and understand many things in life. A good way to do this is by studying and doing homework while you're young and in school.

Doing homework makes you smart and that makes you interesting to other people. So if you do your homework, it will make you smarter, more interesting, and it will help you later in life.

Mark the score that this paper should receive in the trait of VOICE. Read your rubric for Voice to help you decide. Then write your reason for the score.

____ 1 ____ 2 ____ 3 ____ 4 ____ 5 ____ 6

_____

_____

Compare your score with your partner's. How did you do?

____ We matched **exactly!**

____ We matched within **one point**—pretty good!

____ We were **two points or more** apart. We need to discuss this.

Sample Paper 12: My Brother the Pain

Objective

Students will learn that strong feelings make for strong voice and that a paper that holds a reader's interest usually has strong voice.

Materials

Student Rubric for Voice (Teacher's Guide page 41)

Sample Paper 12: My Brother the Pain (Teacher's Guide page 155 and/or Overhead 12)

Scoring the Paper

1. Distribute copies of the sample paper and the Student Rubric for Voice. Use the rubric to focus students' attention on the key features of the trait of VOICE. In particular, students should look and listen for energy, liveliness, or individuality—a paper that truly stands out from others.

2. Have students think about these questions as they listen to you read the paper: *Do you think the writer enjoyed writing the paper? How can you tell?*

3. Ask students to score the paper *individually,* using the rubric. They should mark their scores in writing, putting an **X** in the appropriate blank. (If students do not have copies of the sample paper, they can write on separate sheets of paper.)

4. Ask students to compare their responses with those of a partner. They should take a few minutes to talk about the paper and ask each other questions. Expect this process to be slow at first; they will talk more and come to agreement faster as time goes on.

Discussing the Paper

Discuss the paper with the class. Ask students to say what scores they gave the paper and why. The *why* is the most important part in deepening their understanding. Use the following questions to encourage discussion:

• How does the writer feel about his brother? How can you tell?

• Would you want this story to go on for several more pages? Why or why not?

• Would you want to read another piece by the same writer? Why or why not?

• Would you read this paper aloud to a friend? Explain.

• What word(s) would you use to describe this writer's voice?

Rationale for the Score*

Most students should see this paper as **strong.** It is rich with voice—full of humor and energy. It received a score of **6** on the 6-point rubric. Details enhance the voice, and it's a paper a reader would not mind reading more than once. Even better, the voice is consistent throughout the piece. Some moments may be stronger than others, but the voice never fades.

Extensions

1. Ask each student to write a short paragraph putting these same characters in another situation: The older brother needs to supervise his younger brother at a swimming pool party; the younger brother hits a home run on the same day the older brother strikes out. You may wish to suggest other situations.

2. Have each student look at a piece of his or her own writing and underline any words that are weak or overused. On their own or in pairs, students can brainstorm more descriptive and precise words. See what this revision does for the overall sound of each paper.

*See Teacher's Guide page 197 for a 5-point rubric and page 210 for the score.

My Brother the Pain

My brother has reached that age when he's almost too old to want to hang out with me. He's fourteen, and I'm ten, but those four years in between might as well be forty. It's not like he never talks to me or goofs around with me. He just won't do those things when we are with someone else. He's too worried about his friends and what they want to do. Right now, they mostly want to talk about girls. I hide behind the fence when his friends come over to shoot hoops. After a few minutes, there's very little hoop shooting going on—trust me. They start talking about all these girls they like. They all try to sound so cool—as though they know so much about girls and relationships. I know he sees these girls at school, but I've never seen one girl with him. He's always with his buddies—you know, "the guys." There are some girls who call him at home, but he hardly says a word to them when he gets on the phone. He can barely make up a sentence to say back to them. What I hear are mostly grunts and "yeahs." It sounds as if it's painful for him to talk to them. He's so cool, I actually feel sorry for him.

Mark the score that this paper should receive in the trait of VOICE. Read your rubric for Voice to help you decide.

___ 1 ___ 2 ___ 3 ___ 4 ___ 5 ___ 6

Compare your score with your partner's. How did you do?

___ We matched **exactly!**

___ We matched within **one point**—pretty good!

___ We were **two points or more** apart. We need to discuss this.

Sample Paper 13: Engine

Objective

Students will learn that when a writer uses interesting words correctly, writing is clear and fun to read.

Materials

Student Rubric for Word Choice (Teacher's Guide page 59)

Sample Paper 13: Engine (Teacher's Guide page 158 and/or Overhead 13)

Scoring the Paper

1. Distribute copies of the sample paper and the Student Rubric for Word Choice. Use the rubric to focus students' attention on the key features of the trait of WORD CHOICE. In particular, students should look and listen for strong verbs, sensory words (words that show how things look, sound, smell, taste, and feel), and words that are vague or overused.

2. Have students think about these questions as they listen to you read the paper: *Does the writer use strong verbs? Are any words overused?*

3. Ask students to score the paper *individually,* using the rubric. They should mark their scores in writing, putting an **X** in the appropriate blank. (If students do not have copies of the sample paper, they can write on separate sheets of paper.)

4. Ask students to compare their responses with those of a partner. They should take a few minutes to talk about the paper and ask each other questions.

Discussing the Paper

Discuss the paper with the class. Ask students to say what scores they gave the paper and why. The *why* is the most important part in deepening their understanding. Use the following questions to encourage discussion:

• Are there examples of good word choice in this paper? If so, what are they?

• Should any words be replaced? Which ones?

• Do the writer's words paint a clear picture of the car's experience?

• Could you make a movie from the content of this paper? Why or why not?

*Rationale for the Score**

Most students should see this paper as fairly **strong.** It received a score of **4** on the 6-point rubric. Though it could use some revision, it does have some good moments, beginning with the very first line: *Vroom! Vroom!* The writer's attempt to reproduce the actual sound of the engine is an example of creative word choice. There are other strong moments, too: *tires screech* and *race out onto the track.* The writer also allows a few tired phrases to creep in, and the paper is in need of some stronger action verbs in places. After a good beginning, the writer relies on modifiers, such as *magnificent* to wrap things up.

Extensions

1. Ask students to revise the conclusion to "Engine." Can they tell the same story using stronger verbs and sensory detail?

2. Review "Engine" once more, looking specifically at verbs. Have students revise, replacing any weak verbs with stronger, more descriptive ones.

3. Have each student look at a piece of his or her own writing and underline any weak or overused words. Ask each student to work with a partner to brainstorm better word choices.

*See Teacher's Guide page 198 for a 5-point rubric and page 211 for the score.

Sample Paper 13: WORD CHOICE

Engine

Vroom! Vroom! My engine starts. I feel my tires screech. I race out onto the track. I see the open road ahead, and I go faster and faster. With the other cars on my tail, I speed to the first turn at 100 mph!

I'm in first place, and the other cars are all behind me. Man, look out! I'm going to win this race. My driver is feeling on top of the world!

I speed down the straightaway, but then—OH NO!! My driver uses the wrong gear, and something happens to my engine. I feel heat, then fire! My tires stop spinning. I slow down. The other cars pass me! My driver did something wrong. Everything around me is broken!!!

Now I have to pull over to the pit, and the mechanic will operate on me! It doesn't look good. As they work on me, I think I'm going to get a new driver. But I don't. It is the same one! Oh well, maybe he has learned his lesson. My fellow cars will be amazed by how I survived! I am the magnificent car! I'll win the next race!

Mark the score that this paper should receive in the trait of WORD CHOICE. Read your rubric for Word Choice to help you decide.

____ 1 ____ 2 ____ 3 ____ 4 ____ 5 ____ 6

Sample Paper 14: King of the Surf

Objective

Students will understand that the use of strong verbs makes writing precise, lively, and interesting.

Materials

Student Rubric for Word Choice (Teacher's Guide page 59)

Sample Paper 14: King of the Surf (Teacher's Guide page 161 and/or Overhead 14)

Scoring the Paper

1. Distribute copies of the sample paper and the Student Rubric for Word Choice. Use the rubric to focus students' attention on the key features of the trait of WORD CHOICE. In particular, students should look and listen for strong verbs, sensory words (words that show how things look, sound, smell, taste, and feel), and words that are vague or overused.

2. Have students think about these questions as they listen to you read the paper: *Does the writer use strong verbs? Are any words overused?*

3. Ask students to score the paper *individually,* using the rubric. They should mark their scores in writing, putting an **X** in the appropriate blank. (If students do not have copies of the sample paper, they can write on separate sheets of paper.)

4. Ask students to compare their responses with those of a partner. They should take a few minutes to talk about the paper and ask each other questions.

Discussing the Paper

Discuss the paper with the class. Ask students to say what scores they gave the paper and why. The *why* is the most important part in deepening their understanding. Use the following questions to encourage discussion:

• Which words in this paper are the most lively and interesting?

• Does the paper contain strong verbs? If so, identify them.

• Does this writing create a clear picture of someone surfing? Could you make a film of this episode? Why or why not?

*Rationale for the Score**

Most students should see this paper as **strong.** It received a **6** on the 6-point rubric. The story could use more sensory detail, yet the verbs (and general wording/phrasing) are strong. Here are a few examples: *sustain major injuries, sharp implements, hit the wave, paddled out, scouting out, whole ocean flipped, plunged . . . like an anchor, scrunched.* This writer is very selective, and the words paint a clear picture. There is little repetition. The combination of clarity and humor produces strong voice.

Extensions

1. Start with any piece of writing in which the verbs are strong. Remove each strong verb, and replace it with a tired, less exciting verb. Then, put the result on the overhead. See whether students can replace each of the weak verbs. Compare the finished piece to the original.

2. Have each student look at a piece of his or her own writing. Tell students to underline passages where strong verbs would add some energy, and have them revise. Each writer should try to make at least *four changes.*

3. Score "King of the Surf" for voice. The score should be high. How does voice relate to word choice? Discuss this.

4. Is the title "King of the Surf" a good example of word choice? Why or why not? Have students think of other titles that are examples of good word choice.

*See Teacher's Guide page 198 for a 5-point rubric and page 211 for the score.

name: .... date: ....

Sample Paper 14: WORD CHOICE

King of the Surf

When you hit the wave just right, life is perfect. I found this out when my family visited Hawaii last summer. Now, if you knew me really well, you'd say "Chad? Surfing? Give me a break. He can't walk down the hall without hurting himself and others." I can sustain major injuries opening my locker. My mother won't even let me set the table because sharp implements are involved. But you should have seen my one fine moment in the world of sports—riding a surfboard.

Sure, I was nervous. But I had to try it. I got my surfboard and paddled out as far as I dared to go, hoping the sharks were busy scouting out the other side of the island. I rode along on my surfboard until I could feel the balance coming. Slowly I stood up. I was doing it! I made an unfortunate blunder, though. I waved. The whole ocean suddenly flipped upside down, and for a second I was hanging in space. Then I plunged into the water like an anchor. I scrunched my eyes shut and held my breath and then—pop! I hit the surface like a whale coming up for air. Later, someone told me how ridiculous I had looked spinning through the air. Did I care? Come on. I was king of the surf for a whole ten seconds.

Mark the score that this paper should receive in the trait of WORD CHOICE. Read your rubric for Word Choice to help you decide.

___ 1 ___ 2 ___ 3 ___ 4 ___ 5 ___ 6

Sample Paper 15: Movies Are My Favorite Thing

Objective

Students will learn to avoid repetition and revise for fresh and original phrasing.

Materials

Student Rubric for Word Choice (Teacher's Guide page 59)

Sample Paper 15: Movies Are My Favorite Thing (Teacher's Guide page 164 and/or Overhead 15)

Scoring the Paper

1. Distribute copies of the sample paper and the Student Rubric for Word Choice. Use the rubric to focus students' attention on the key features of the trait of WORD CHOICE. In particular, students should look and listen for favorite words, strong verbs, sensory words (words that show how things look, sound, smell, taste, and feel), and any words that are vague or overused.

2. Have students think about these questions as they listen to you read the paper: *Does the writer's choice of words help make the subject clear? Are any words vague or overused?*

3. Ask students to score the paper *individually,* using the rubric. They should mark their scores in writing, putting an **X** in the appropriate blank. (If students do not have copies of the sample paper, they can write on separate sheets of paper.)

4. Ask students to compare their responses with those of a partner. They should take a few minutes to talk about the paper and ask each other questions.

5. After three or four minutes, ask students to write their reasons for scoring the paper as they did.

Discussing the Paper

Discuss the paper with the class. Ask students to say what scores they gave the paper and why. The *why* is the most important part in deepening their understanding. Use the following questions to encourage discussion:

- Which words in this paper are your favorites?

- Do you notice any strong verbs? Identify these verbs.

- Are any words overused? If so, what words are they?

- Do the words paint a clear picture in your mind? Explain.

*Rationale for the Score**

Even though the main idea in this paper is clear, most students should see this paper as **weak.** It received a **2** on the 6-point rubric. Words are not misused, but they are certainly overused: for example, *best, huge, really, stuff.* These words tell the reader what is happening, but they show the reader little or nothing. Details are also noticeably missing and so are strong verbs. The paper has potential, but the writer needs to describe the sounds and smells of the theater and the lobby. More sensory detail would greatly improve the paper.

Extensions

1. Have the class brainstorm a list of sensory details that describe what it is like to go to the movies. Make sure students capture the sights, sounds, tastes, smells, and feelings. Then, have them create paragraphs rich with detail, putting the reader right at the scene. Tell students to avoid vague or overused words.

2. Ask each student to review a piece of his or her own writing and delete or replace any vague or overused words.

3. Have students create movie posters featuring their favorite films. Tell them to make the word choice as lively and expressive as possible. You may wish to bring in a movie poster or two as an example. Talk about the kind of language that makes people want to see a film. How different is it from the language in "Movies Are My Favorite Thing"? (Posters can be illustrated with photos from postcards or magazines or with students' sketches.)

*See Teacher's Guide page 198 for a 5-point rubric and page 211 for the score.

Sample Paper 15: WORD CHOICE

Movies Are My Favorite Thing

My favorite thing to do is go to the movies. I would go every day if my mom would let me go. If you have ever been to the movies, you know how fun it is. The best thing about going to the movies is the food. I could eat theater food every day. There's popcorn, which is my favorite thing, and also huge cold drinks, hot dogs, pretzels, and a ton of other stuff. Some of the stuff I don't really like that much, but I like most of it. The candy is the next best thing because there is every kind in the world at the movies, and you can buy a really huge, humongous box that will last you for the whole movie or most of it, anyway. I love the huge seats in the movies. You can sit right in the front, so the screen is really huge. You can see everything. I like that. You get to sit with your friends, and you see a movie you have never seen before. Even if it isn't that good, it is way better than TV, which is old because a lot of the stuff you have already seen. I do not even watch TV that much, but I could go to the movies every single day because it is something I never get tired of.

Mark the score that this paper should receive in the trait of WORD CHOICE. Read your rubric for Word Choice to help you decide. Then write your reason for the score.

___ 1 ___ 2 ___ 3 ___ 4 ___ 5 ___ 6

_____

_____

Sample Paper 16: Life on the Prairie

Objective

Students will understand that misusing words obscures meaning.

Materials

Student Rubric for Word Choice (Teacher's Guide page 59)

Sample Paper 16: Life on the Prairie (Teacher's Guide page 167 and/or Overhead 16)

Scoring the Paper

1. Distribute copies of the sample paper and the Student Rubric for Word Choice. Use the rubric to focus students' attention on the key features of the trait of WORD CHOICE. In particular, students should look and listen for strong verbs, sensory words (words that show how things look, sound, smell, taste, and feel), or any words that are vague or overused. They should also look for words that are misused or unclear from context.

2. Have students think about these questions as they listen to you read the paper: *Are all the words used correctly? Does the writer's choice of words help you understand the main idea?*

3. Ask students to score the paper *individually,* using the rubric. They should mark their scores in writing, putting an **X** in the appropriate blank. (If students do not have copies of the sample paper, they can write on separate sheets of paper.)

4. Ask students to compare their responses with those of a partner. They should take a few minutes to talk about the paper and ask each other questions.

Discussing the Paper

Discuss the paper with the class. Ask students to say what scores they gave the paper and why. The *why* is the most important part in deepening their understanding. Use the following questions to encourage discussion:

• Did you learn much about life on the prairie from this paper?

• Were any words unclear? Which ones?

• Are some words misused? Which ones?

• Would you replace any words? Which ones?

*Rationale for the Score**

Most students should see this paper as fairly **weak.** It received a **2** on the 6-point rubric. Many words are misused, making meaning unclear: for example, *frantic, eradicated, surly (surly* stew?), *selective (selective* floors?), *abundant, pauperized* (overkill for *poor)*. These misused words obscure meaning. The writer does use one strong verb: *eradicated.* Unfortunately, it is not used correctly—snakes certainly did not *eradicate* the pioneers, and *eradicating* people from their homes does not make sense. This writer is trying hard to breathe some life into the writing, but he or she has simply used too many words incorrectly.

Extensions

1. Have each student work with a partner. Tell partners to underline the words in "Life on the Prairie" that are used incorrectly or whose meaning is unclear. Ask each student pair to use a dictionary to find the definitions for the underlined words and to replace them with more appropriate word choices.

2. Tell each student to write a note to this writer, offering some advice on word choice. Be sure that students understand that the writer is trying to use a sophisticated vocabulary.

*See Teacher's Guide page 198 for a 5-point rubric and page 212 for the score.

Sample Paper 16: WORD CHOICE

Life on the Prairie

The pioneers had turbulent lives. Their lives were frantic, much like ours today, except that they did not have the conveniences of stores and other appliances. Life on the prairie could be very harsh and eradicated many of the settlers from their homes. Many died. Snakes eradicated many of the pioneers as well.

The pioneers' meals were meager and not very nutritious. They had surly stew and sour biscuits. These foods were harsh to live on for any length of time. Many of the pioneers suffered from diseases as a result of their poor diets.

Their homes were not much better. Unlike the homes of today, pioneer homes did not always have windows. And floors were pretty selective, usually consisting only of plain dirt which was difficult to clean.

Travel was abundant but difficult and treacherous with horses and wagons being the main means of transportation. Many pioneers were pauperized and could not afford wagons. This could mean a long, harsh journey to the land of their dreams.

Mark the score that this paper should receive in the trait of WORD CHOICE. Read your rubric for Word Choice to help you decide.

___ 1 ___ 2 ___ 3 ___ 4 ___ 5 ___ 6

Sentence Fluency

Sample Paper 17: Alligator

Objective

Students will learn to avoid long, rambling, and repetitive sentences.

Materials

Student Rubric for Sentence Fluency (Teacher's Guide page 77)

Sample Paper 17: Alligator (Teacher's Guide page 170 and/or Overhead 17)

Scoring the Paper

1. Distribute copies of the sample paper and the Student Rubric for Sentence Fluency. Use the rubric to focus students' attention on the key features of the trait of SENTENCE FLUENCY. In particular, students should look and listen for differences in sentence beginnings and sentence lengths, run-ons or rambling sentences, natural dialogue, and a smooth flow of ideas.

2. Have students think about these questions as they listen to you read the paper: *Does the writer vary the sentence beginnings? Are there any run-on sentences?*

3. Ask students to score the paper *individually,* using the rubric. They should mark their scores in writing, putting an **X** in the appropriate blank. (If students do not have copies of the sample paper, they can write on separate sheets of paper.)

4. Ask students to compare their responses with those of a partner. They should take a few minutes to talk about the paper and ask each other questions.

5. After three or four minutes, ask students to write their reasons for scoring the paper as they did.

Discussing the Paper

Discuss the paper with the class. Ask students to say what scores they gave the paper and why. The *why* is the most important part in deepening their understanding. Use the following questions to encourage discussion:

- As you looked and listened to this paper, what did you notice about the sentence beginnings? Did the sentence beginnings help or hurt the fluency?

- Did you notice any run-on sentences or rambling sentences—sentences that go on and on with too many connecting words? Did these sentences help or hurt the fluency?

- Is it hard to read this paper aloud? Do you need to practice? Why?

*Rationale for the Score**

Most students should see this paper as **weak.** It received a **2** on the 6-point rubric because the sentences are long, rambling, and repetitive. This makes the writer sound breathless! It is difficult to make this paper sound smooth without some rehearsal. With some sentence reconstruction and attention to varied beginnings, this could be a very strong paper. The writer has used some imagination, but the paragraph needs revision.

Extensions

1. "Alligator" is a good paper to revise as a class. Work on one problem at a time. First, ask students to suggest ways to revise the sentences. Then have them work on writing varied sentence beginnings. You can brainstorm two or three possibilities, and then settle on the ones the class likes best. Finally, read the revised paragraph aloud. You should hear considerable improvement.

2. Organize students in groups of four for round-table sentence construction. The first student in each group will begin a story or essay by writing one sentence. (Rule: Students cannot begin a sentence with *So, Then, I,* or *We.*) The next student will continue the story or essay by writing another sentence with a different beginning. Have group members continue writing new sentences until each of them has written three sentences. Have a volunteer from each group read that group's sentences aloud. Did students vary their sentence beginnings? Did they vary the length of their sentences? Do the sentences connect to create a coherent story or essay?

*See Teacher's Guide page 199 for a 5-point rubric and page 212 for the score.

Sample Paper 17: SENTENCE FLUENCY

Alligator

I started to open the bathroom door when I heard the bathtub water running, and I started to yell, "Who is it?" I thought it was a strange time for someone in my family to be taking a bath, so I looked in. I saw an alligator trying to get in the bathtub, so I ran, and got everyone gathered up, and I whispered to everyone, "I saw an alligator trying to get in the tub, so let's help him so he can get clean." So everyone helped wash him and from that day on, we have let him stay.

Mark the score that this paper should receive in the trait of SENTENCE FLUENCY. Read your rubric for Sentence Fluency to help you decide. Then write your reason for the score.

___ 1 ___ 2 ___ 3 ___ 4 ___ 5 ___ 6

_____

_____

Compare your score with your partner's. How did you do?

____ We matched **exactly!**

____ We matched within **one point**—pretty good!

____ We were **two points or more** apart. We need to discuss this.

Sample Paper 18: Chinese Dragon

Objective

Students will understand that when sentences begin in different ways and dialogue sounds natural, fluency increases.

Materials

Student Rubric for Sentence Fluency (Teacher's Guide page 77)

Sample Paper 18: Chinese Dragon (Teacher's Guide pages 173–174 and/or Overheads 18–18a)

Scoring the Paper

1. Distribute copies of the sample paper and the Student Rubric for Sentence Fluency. Use the rubric to focus students' attention on the key features of the trait of SENTENCE FLUENCY. In particular, students should look and listen for differences in sentence beginnings and sentence lengths, run-ons or rambling sentences, natural dialogue, and a smooth flow of ideas.

2. Have students think about these questions as they listen to you read the paper: *Are the sentence lengths varied? Does the dialogue sound natural?*

3. Ask students to score the paper *individually,* using the rubric. They should mark their scores in writing, putting an **X** in the appropriate blank. (If students do not have copies of the sample paper, they can write on separate sheets of paper.)

4. Ask students to compare their responses with those of a partner. They should take a few minutes to talk about the paper and ask each other questions. Expect this process to be slow at first; they will talk more and come to agreement faster as time goes on.

5. After three or four minutes, ask students to write their reasons for scoring the paper as they did.

Discussing the Paper

Discuss the paper with the class. Ask students to say what scores they gave the paper and why. The *why* is the most important part in deepening their understanding. Use the following questions to encourage discussion:

- As you looked and listened to this paper, what did you notice about the sentence beginnings? Did the sentence beginnings help or hurt the fluency?

- Did you think the paper sounded smooth when you heard it read aloud, or was it a little choppy? Do you think you could read it aloud without difficulty?

- Notice the dialogue between the writer and the dragon. Do you think the conversation sounds natural? Why or why not?

*Rationale for the Score**

Most students should see this paper as **strong.** It received a **5** on the 6-point rubric. Sentences are varied, the dialogue is believable, and the piece is easy to read. The language is natural, not stilted or phony. Students will have an easy time reading this paper aloud.

Extensions

1. Invite students to score this paper for the trait of IDEAS. These scores probably will not be as high as those for *sentence fluency*. Though the paper is highly imaginative and includes some good details, it does leave some important questions unanswered. You may wish to have students brainstorm a list of unanswered questions and try revising the paper to answer them.

2. Have students extend the dialogue between Charizard and the narrator to answer some questions: How did Charizard find the narrator? Why does Charizard love China? Why must he live in a royal zoo?

*See Teacher's Guide page 199 for a 5-point rubric and page 212 for the score.

Sample Paper 18: SENTENCE FLUENCY

Chinese Dragon

I was just putting the finishing touches on my Chinese dragon in art class when something extraordinary happened. The lights in the room flickered and suddenly went out. When the lights came back on, a huge dragon was sitting on the table in front of me.

"Uh, hello," I mumbled.

"Errrp!" burped the dragon.

"What kind of greeting is a burp?" I asked.

"I'm sorry. I just had lunch," he admitted. The dragon just stared at me and said nothing more.

Over the next couple of days that dragon and I became very good friends. There was a problem, though. The dragon started to become homesick. Charizard (he told me his name) wanted to go back to his home, which was in China. We talked about it and decided that there was only one thing to do. Charizard would have to go back home.

I told him that we were a very long way from China and that it would probably take years for him to walk home. It was then that he told me a secret—he could fly! I rode on Charizard's back as we flew on our journey to his homeland. What a sight we must have been. We had such a fun time visiting different places and getting our pictures taken along the way.

Finally we arrived in China. As was customary, Charizard had to be placed in the Emperor's royal zoo. I got to visit him every week, though. The Emperor treated me as though I were family. Charizard was happy to be where he was, and I was happy, too.

Mark the score that this paper should receive in the trait of SENTENCE FLUENCY. Read your rubric for Sentence Fluency to help you decide. Then write your reason for the score.

___ 1 ___ 2 ___ 3 ___ 4 ___ 5 ___ 6

_____

_____

Compare your score with your partner's. How did you do?

___ We matched **exactly!**

___ We matched within **one point**—pretty good!

___ We were **two points or more** apart. We need to discuss this.

Sample Paper 19: Flying

Objective

Students will recognize that well-crafted, varied sentences can create a smooth flow of ideas that is pleasing to read and hear.

Materials

Student Rubric for Sentence Fluency (Teacher's Guide page 77)

Sample Paper 19: Flying (Teacher's Guide page 177 and/or Overhead 19)

Scoring the Paper

1. Distribute copies of the sample paper and the Student Rubric for Sentence Fluency. Use the rubric to focus students' attention on the key features of the trait of SENTENCE FLUENCY. In particular, students should look and listen for differences in sentence beginnings and sentence lengths, run-ons or rambling sentences, natural dialogue, and a smooth flow of ideas.

2. Have students think about this question as they listen to you read the paper: *Does the writing sound smooth when read aloud?*

3. Ask students to score the paper *individually,* using the rubric. They should mark their scores in writing, putting an **X** in the appropriate blank. (If students do not have copies of the sample paper, they can write on separate sheets of paper.)

4. Ask students to compare their responses with those of a partner. They should take a few minutes to talk about the paper and ask each other questions.

Discussing the Paper

Discuss the paper with the class. Ask students to say what scores they gave the paper and why. The *why* is the most important part in deepening their understanding. Use the following questions to encourage discussion:

- As you looked at and listened to this paper, what did you notice about the sentence beginnings? How was fluency affected by sentence beginnings?

- Did the paper sound smooth when it was read aloud?

- Would reading this paper aloud be easy or difficult? Explain.

- Do the sentences vary in length? How does sentence length affect fluency?

*Rationale for the Score**

Most students should see this paper as **strong.** It received a **6** on the 6-point rubric because virtually all of the sentences begin differently, it has no troublesome fluency problems, and the sentences read smoothly. It's a pleasure to read aloud. In addition, the sentences are highly varied in length. The writer does include some fragments, but these enhance the style and voice.

Extensions

1. Ask two or three volunteers to read "Flying" aloud. Have the rest of the class close their eyes and listen. What do they hear? Do they think this paragraph is strong in sentence fluency?

2. Have students read pieces of their own writing to one another in response groups. They should listen *only* for sentence fluency. Remind them to pay attention to sentence beginnings and lengths. They should NOT hear any run-ons or rambling sentences.

3. Have students work with partners. Ask them to identify sentence fragments in "Flying." After they have identified sentence fragments, ask students whether they think the fragments sound appropriate in this piece. Explain that using fragments requires skill; fragments can make a piece of writing ungrammatical and difficult to understand.

*See Teacher's Guide page 199 for a 5-point rubric and page 213 for the score.

name: .... date: ....

Sample Paper 19: SENTENCE FLUENCY

Flying

Flying is designed for small, flexible, patient people. If these words do not describe you, stay far away from airplanes. Take the bus. Drive. Stay home. Do anything except get on the plane. The first thing you'll discover about flying is that the rule about "one carry-on bag per passenger" applies to YOU. That's right. Everyone else has three giant bags that look big enough to hold a hippopotamus or two. The biggest test of your patience comes when you try to sit down and buckle yourself in. Better get your feet right where you want them because you won't get a chance to change your mind. The seat in front of you is probably rubbing your knees, and when you can't stand it for one more minute, the guy in front of you decides to lean back for a snooze. Want to enjoy the airline lunch? First, pull down your tray. It punches conveniently into your ribs. Chicken a little tough? Would you like to cut it? Too bad, because you would need to move your elbows to do that, and you cannot move your elbows on the airplane—not the way you're jammed into that seat. People always carry on about the convenience of flying. I'd give up some of the convenience for some comfort.

Mark the score that this paper should receive in the trait of SENTENCE FLUENCY. Read your rubric for Sentence Fluency to help you decide.

___ 1 ___ 2 ___ 3 ___ 4 ___ 5 ___ 6

Sample Paper 20: Shopping

Objective

Students will recognize that varied sentence structure and realistic dialogue give writing fluency.

Materials

Student Rubric for Sentence Fluency (Teacher's Guide page 77)

Sample Paper 20: Shopping (Teacher's Guide page 180 and/or Overhead 20)

Scoring the Paper

1. Distribute copies of the sample paper and the Student Rubric for Sentence Fluency. Use the rubric to focus students' attention on the key features of the trait of SENTENCE FLUENCY. In particular, students should look and listen for differences in sentence beginnings and sentence lengths, run-ons or rambling sentences, natural dialogue, and a smooth flow of ideas.

2. Have students think about these questions as they listen to you read aloud the paper: *Are sentence beginnings varied? Are the sentences smooth, or will the reader stumble over choppy sentences?*

3. Ask students to score the paper *individually,* using the rubric. They should mark their scores in writing, putting an **X** in the appropriate blank. (If students do not have copies of the sample paper, they can write on separate sheets of paper.)

4. Ask students to compare their responses with those of a partner. They should take a few minutes to talk about the paper and ask each other questions.

5. After three or four minutes, ask students to write their reasons for scoring the paper as they did.

Discussing the Paper

Discuss the paper with the class. Ask students to say what scores they gave the paper and why. The *why* is the most important part in deepening their understanding. Use the following questions to encourage discussion:

• Do many sentences in this paper begin differently? What effect does this have on the fluency?

• Does this paper sound smooth read aloud? Why or why not?

• Are many sentences similar in length? If so, how does this similarity affect fluency?

• Does the dialogue sound like two people having a conversation?

• What would you do to improve the fluency of this paper?

*Rationale for the Score**

Most students should see this paper as somewhat **weak.** It received a **3** on the 6-point rubric because the sentences tend to be choppy. Also, many sentences are the same length, and many have similar beginnings as well. The dialogue between the parents does not emphasize the differences between their approaches to shopping. Some revision of sentence lengths and beginnings will give this paper the fluency it needs.

Extensions

1. Have students work with partners. Ask them to revise "Shopping" for fluency. They should be acquainted with the possibilities for revision on this trait, so let them work out their own plans for revision.

2. Have students create extended dialogues between the parents from "Shopping." Point out that the dialogues should emphasize each character's approach to shopping as well as each character's frustrations with the other's approach to shopping. Ask students to perform their new dialogues for the class.

3. Have students brainstorm lists of things people do in individual ways: homework, driving, preparing food, cleaning, and so on. Ask each student to select one item from the list and write a comparison-contrast paragraph explaining two different approaches to one process. Have volunteers read their paragraphs aloud. Be sure to write a comparison-contrast paper of your own.

*See Teacher's Guide page 199 for a 5-point rubric and page 213 for the score.

Sample Paper 20: SENTENCE FLUENCY

Shopping

All people don't shop the same way. My dad always makes a list. He follows the list to the letter. He doesn't buy a single thing that is not on the list. That is the way he likes to do it. My mom just goes up and down the aisles. She loads up her grocery cart with anything that catches her eye. My dad can't believe all the stuff she buys. My dad says, "Why did you buy this?" My mom says, "Oh, I don't know." My dad says, "Well, I think we already have cereal." My mom says, "I am pretty sure we're out." My dad and my mom shop differently. I think a shopping list is a good idea.

Mark the score that this paper should receive in the trait of SENTENCE FLUENCY. Read your rubric for Sentence Fluency to help you decide. Then write your reason for the score.

___ 1 ___ 2 ___ 3 ___ 4 ___ 5 ___ 6

_____

_____

Compare your score with your partner's. How did you do?

____ We matched **exactly!**

____ We matched within **one point**—pretty good!

____ We were **two points or more** apart. We need to discuss this.

[Conventions]

Sample Paper 21: Flank Steak and Other Treats

Objective

Students will understand that papers strong in conventions help readers' comprehension.

Materials

Student Rubric for Conventions (Teacher's Guide page 95)

Sample Paper 21: Flank Steak and Other Treats (Teacher's Guide page 183 and/or Overhead 21)

Scoring the Paper

1. Distribute copies of the sample paper and the Student Rubric for Conventions. Use the rubric to focus students' attention on the key features of the trait of CONVENTIONS. In particular, students should look and listen for missing or repeated words and any errors in spelling, punctuation, grammar, and capitalization.

2. Have students think about these questions as they listen to you read the paper: *Do you think this writer edited the paper? How can you tell?*

3. Ask students to score the paper *individually,* using the rubric. They should mark their scores in writing, putting an **X** in the appropriate blank. (If students do not have copies of the sample paper, they can write on separate sheets of paper.)

4. Ask students to compare their responses with those of a partner. They should take a few minutes to talk about the paper and ask each other questions.

5. After three or four minutes, ask students to write their reasons for scoring the paper as they did.

Discussing the Paper

Discuss the paper with the class. Ask students to say what scores they gave the paper and why. The *why* is the most important part in deepening their understanding. Use the following questions to encourage discussion:

- As you read through this paper, did you notice many errors? a few errors? almost no errors?

- Do the mistakes this writer made slow your reading? If so, at what points do you slow down?

- Is this piece ready to publish? Why?

*Rationale for the Score**

Most students should see this paper as **strong.** It received a **6** on the 6-point rubric because it contains virtually no errors. This writer has done an excellent job of handling conventions effectively and making the text easy to read.

Extensions

1. Because this text does not contain many errors, there's little point in editing it further. However, you may wish to invite students to identify some of the things this writer does correctly. Make a list of these items for students to consider.

2. Invite students to look at pieces of their own writing and circle any errors they find. Later, they can go back and make corrections.

3. Did students identify any "errors" in this piece that were not really errors? Students may have *thought* something was done incorrectly. Be sure to take time to discuss these items, using examples as necessary.

*See Teacher's Guide page 200 for a 5-point rubric and page 213 for the score.

Sample Paper 21: CONVENTIONS

Flank Steak and Other Treats

Flank steak, chicken noodle soup, and pretzels are my favorite foods. I like my dad's steak the best. I love every tender morsel as it melts in my mouth. I also love the wonderful smell it gives off when my dad puts more marinade on it. Everyone should try my dad's steak.

I love pretzels almost as much as I love flank steak. I love the crispy, salty sticks as I chew them into pretzel dust. I also love how each pretzel seems to have a different texture. I know this because I've been eating them all of my life. I will pass up chocolate anytime if I can have a pretzel instead.

If you've ever been sick, you know how good chicken noodle soup tastes. I love chicken noodle soup because its hot, salty, steamy broth is delectable! I can't forget the warmth of the first spoonful. I really love chicken noodle soup. I think these three foods will be my favorites for a long time.

Mark the score that this paper should receive in the trait of CONVENTIONS. Read your rubric for Conventions to help you decide. Then write your reason for the score.

___ 1 ___ 2 ___ 3 ___ 4 ___ 5 ___ 6

_____

_____

Sample Paper 22: A Career in Nursing

Objective

Students will recognize that errors in conventions slow reading rates and sometimes get in the way of the writer's message.

Materials

Student Rubric for Conventions (Teacher's Guide page 95)

Sample Paper 22: A Career in Nursing (Teacher's Guide page 186 and/or Overhead 22)

Scoring the Paper

1. Distribute copies of the sample paper and the Student Rubric for Conventions. Use the rubric to focus students' attention on the key features of the trait of CONVENTIONS. In particular, students should look and listen for missing or repeated words and any errors in spelling, punctuation, grammar, and capitalization.

2. Have students think about these questions as they listen to you read the paper: *Are there many errors in this paper? Does the number of errors affect the reader's understanding of the writer's message?*

3. Ask students to score the paper *individually,* using the rubric. They should mark their scores in writing, putting an **X** in the appropriate blank. (If students do not have copies of the sample paper, they can write on separate sheets of paper.)

4. Ask students to compare their responses with those of a partner. They should take a few minutes to talk about the paper and ask each other questions.

5. After three or four minutes, ask students to write their reasons for scoring the paper as they did.

Discussing the Paper

Discuss the paper with the class. Ask students to say what scores they gave the paper and why. The *why* is the most important part in deepening their understanding. Use the following questions to encourage discussion:

- As you read through this paper, did you notice many errors? a few errors? almost no errors?

- Did the mistakes in this piece slow your reading? Did they get in the way of the writer's message? If so, where?

- How much work would it take to get this paper ready for publication?

*Rationale for the Score**

Most students should see this paper as **weak.** It received a **2** on the 6-point rubric because it contains many errors. The errors would slow a careful reader.

Extensions

1. Ask students to count the number of errors they circled in "A Career in Nursing." Construct a continuum, and have students vote for one of the following: *many errors, some errors, a few errors,* or *no errors.*

2. Have student partners edit the text. When students have finished editing, have them help you identify the errors. Explain any changes that students do not understand.

*See Teacher's Guide page 200 for a 5-point rubric and page 213 for the score.

Sample Paper 22: CONVENTIONS

A Career in Nursing

I am thiking of becoming nurse wen i go to college I do do not no for sure yet if this is what I really want to do but it is one idea. Nurses help people alot. Thats one thing that really appeal to me. Of corse, nurse also have to do some hard things such drawing blood. I think the needles mite bother me

Mark the score that this paper should receive in the trait of CONVENTIONS. Read your rubric for Conventions to help you decide. Then write your reason for the score.

____ 1 ____ 2 ____ 3 ____ 4 ____ 5 ____ 6

_____

_____

Compare your score with your partner's. How did you do?

____ We matched **exactly!**

____ We matched within **one point**—pretty good!

____ We were **two points or more** apart. We need to discuss this.

Sample Paper 23: The Best Hideout

Objective

Students will recognize that errors in conventions slow reading and may divert attention from the writer's message.

Materials

Student Rubric for Conventions (Teacher's Guide page 95)

Sample Paper 23: The Best Hideout (Teacher's Guide page 189 and/or Overhead 23)

Scoring the Paper

1. Distribute copies of the sample paper and the Student Rubric for Conventions. Use the rubric to focus students' attention on the key features of the trait of CONVENTIONS. In particular, students should look and listen for missing or repeated words and any errors in spelling, punctuation, grammar, and capitalization.

2. Have students think about these questions as they listen to you read the paper: *Are there many errors in this paper? Does the number of errors affect the reader's understanding of the writer's message?*

3. Ask students to score the paper *individually,* using the rubric. They should mark their scores in writing, putting an **X** in the appropriate blank. (If students do not have copies of the sample paper, they can write on separate sheets of paper.)

4. Ask students to compare their responses with those of a partner. They should take a few minutes to talk about the paper and ask each other questions.

Discussing the Paper

Discuss the paper with the class. Ask students to say what scores they gave the paper and why. The *why* is the most important part in deepening their understanding. Use the following questions to encourage discussion:

- As you read through this paper, did you notice many errors? a few errors? almost no errors?
- Is there any place in this paper where errors in conventions slow your reading?
- Is this paper ready for publication? Why or why not?
- Does this writer's use of conventions make the paper easy to read?

*Rationale for the Score**

Most students should see this paper as somewhat **strong.** It received a **4** on the 6-point rubric because the errors do not impair readability. The errors tend to be small—a missing word, a repeated word, a missing apostrophe, and so on. On the other hand, the writer is not fully in control of conventions, and moderate editing would be needed to prepare this piece for publication.

Extensions

1. Ask students to edit "The Best Hideout." Students should find every error, if possible. Have students edit individually first and then work with partners.

2. As students look over this piece of writing, have them identify any patterns in the kinds of errors this writer is making. Ask them to draft letters of advice, giving this writer some tips on successful editing. What would help?

3. Ask each student to use the errors in this paper as models and write a conventions quiz: one sentence containing just ONE error. They can make the quizzes as tricky as they like! Then, ask them to exchange sentences with partners to see whether they can find and correct each other's errors. When everyone is finished, share quizzes. Find out who had the toughest, trickiest error to find and correct.

*See Teacher's Guide page 200 for a 5-point rubric and page 214 for the score.

Sample Paper 23: CONVENTIONS

The Best Hideout

If you want a place to just get away from the hole world, a tree houses is tough to beat. You can built your own, which is what I recommend. If you use someone elses, its not the same. You don't need that much wood. Tree houses don't need walls In fact, I think it spoils the whole efect, which is to see the world from your own perch. You do need a sturdy base, and you might need an adult to help you hamer in a couple of tough boards. The hardest part is finding the right spot. My tree house is in a clump of three trees, which is perfect. Each tree has a foundation board on it, and then I built a square box shaped platform on top that and nailed the floor on top of that. It's three layers altogether. It doesn't have any walls or a roof, but the floor had a rug made out of thick carpet my mom bought at garage sale. I have a shelf for books, a flashlight, a jar for creatures I catch, and some cookies. You need food in a hideout. Above the shelf there a sign, "Jack's Tree House—Keep Out!" It doesn't mean anything, really, because I let everyone in. i have a rope ladder to get up, and once your in, you can pull it up if you don't want visitors, but I usually don't do that, except to my sister.

Mark the score that this paper should receive in the trait of CONVENTIONS. Read your rubric for Conventions to help you decide.

—— 1 —— 2 —— 3 —— 4 —— 5 —— 6

Sample Paper 24: Pizza Mania

Objective

Students will understand that proper use of conventions promotes fluency and reading comprehension.

Materials

Student Rubric for Conventions (Teacher's Guide page 95)

Sample Paper 24: Pizza Mania (Teacher's Guide page 192 and/or Overhead 24)

Scoring the Paper

1. Distribute copies of the sample paper and the Student Rubric for Conventions. Use the rubric to focus students' attention on the key features of the trait of CONVENTIONS. In particular, students should look and listen for missing or repeated words and any errors in spelling, punctuation, grammar, and capitalization.

2. Have students think about these questions as they listen to you read the paper: *Are there many errors in this paper? Does the number of errors affect the reader's understanding of the writer's message?*

3. Ask students to score the paper *individually,* using the rubric. They should mark their scores in writing, putting an **X** in the appropriate blank. (If students do not have copies of the sample paper, they can write on separate sheets of paper.)

4. Ask students to compare their responses with those of a partner. They should take a few minutes to talk about the paper and ask each other questions.

Discussing the Paper

Discuss the paper with the class. Ask students to say what scores they gave the paper and why. The *why* is the most important part in deepening their understanding. Use the following questions to encourage discussion:

• As you read through this paper, did you notice many errors? a few errors? almost no errors?

• Do this paper's errors in conventions slow your reading? If so, at what points?

• Do you think this paper is ready for publication? Why or why not?

*Rationale for the Score**

Most students should see this paper as **weak.** It received a **2** on the 6-point rubric because it contains many errors in conventions, making reading difficult. It needs serious editorial review.

Extensions

1. Have students work in groups to edit "Pizza Mania" for conventions. Because the paper contains so many errors, divide the project by giving each group one or two sentences to revise. Have the students review edited drafts, and discuss with them the reasons for any corrections.

2. Create a draft on the overhead on any topic your students select for you. Then, as you write the paper, occasionally slip in an error in conventions. See how quickly students can identify each error as you write.

3. Score "Pizza Mania" for other traits. Scores will probably improve, especially for voice. Read the paper aloud, asking students to follow along.

*See Teacher's Guide page 200 for a 5-point rubric and page 214 for the score.

Sample Paper 24: CONVENTIONS
Pizza Mania

My mom says you can make piza out of anything one night she set out to prove it. We had a basic cheese pizza in the freexer. Take it from me, we should have just gone with that. Instead she starts rummaging thru the fridge to see what else she could fine to goes on top. she came up with leftover chili, some spaghetti sause, pickles, and shrimp i hate shrimp. Then she goes added some artichokes. Thats when I said, OK, I'm not eating that." She said, Don't worry You'll love it. I thought she saw crazy. You know whats? It wasn't all all too that bad. It was just a good thing we ate by candle light, thought, so you couldn't really tell see one lump from another. I hop my mom never opening a restaurant. Peoples could get sick.

Mark the score that this paper should receive in the trait of CONVENTIONS. Read your rubric for Conventions to help you decide.

___ 1 ___ 2 ___ 3 ___ 4 ___ 5 ___ 6

Compare your score with your partner's. How did you do?

___ We matched **exactly!**

___ We matched within **one point**—pretty good!

___ We were **two points or more** apart. We need to discuss this.

Appendix:

Using a 5-Point Rubric

For your convenience, we have included in this appendix 5-point student and teacher rubrics for each trait and a score for each Sample Paper based on the 5-point rubric. Although we have always recommended the 6-point rubric, the 5-point rubric has certain advantages.

The 5-point rubric is easy to use and to internalize. Performance is defined at only three levels: **weak** (point 1), **somewhat strong** (point 3), and **strong** or proficient (point 5). The 4 and the 2 on the 5-point rubric are compromise scores. Therefore, if a performance is slightly stronger than a 3 but not quite strong enough to warrant a 5, it would receive a 4. Because raters think in terms of "weak, somewhat strong, and strong" in assigning scores, this is a simple system to follow.

Performance in writing is defined at only three levels, so it is possible to make those written definitions longer and more detailed than when defining *every* level. Many users like this richer text, especially if they are learning traits for the first time or if they are looking for language to use in teaching traits to students.

Few differences exist conceptually between these rubrics. Remember that the key reason to use rubrics with students is to teach the concepts: *ideas, organization, voice, word choice, sentence fluency,* and *conventions.* We want students to understand what we mean, for example, by good *organization,* and one way of doing this is to have them score writing samples. The particular rubric used is less important than whether a student sees a paper as weak, strong, or somewhere between those two points. We want students to distinguish between writing that works and writing that needs revision; whether they define a strong performance as a 5 or 6 is much less important than their understanding of why a paper is strong or weak. The numbers are merely a kind of shorthand that allows students and teachers to discuss competency in simple terms.

Keep in mind, too, that all rubrics are essentially 3-point rubrics: weak, somewhat strong, and strong. On the 5-point rubric, these performance levels correspond to the scores of 1, 3, and 5 respectively. On the 6-point rubric, each level is divided into two parts, high and low. Thus, a score of 1 represents the lowest weak score, a score of 2 is a somewhat higher weak score, and so on. Scores of 3 and 4 represent the two levels of the somewhat strong category, 5 and 6 the two levels of strength. On the 6-point rubric, *all* performance levels are defined.

We hope that these distinctions help clarify the very slight differences between these rubrics. Use the rubrics with which you are most familiar or with which you feel most comfortable. Regardless of your choice, you will be teaching your students about the basic components that define good writing—and that is what counts!

Ideas

5 My paper has details that make my main idea clear.

- Readers can tell that I know a lot about this topic.

- It's easy to determine my main idea.

- I chose my details carefully. They are important and interesting.

- I left out the "filler."

3 My paper is clear in some parts, but I need more information. My details are too general.

- I know some things about this topic. I wish I knew more.

- Readers can identify my main idea.

- Some of my "details" are things most people already know.

- Some information is not needed. It's just filler.

- This topic feels big—maybe I'm trying to tell too much.

1 I'm still working on what I want to say.

- Help! I don't know enough about this topic to write about it.

- Can readers identify my main idea? I'm not sure myself!

- I need better details. I just tossed in anything I could think of.

- I was writing to fill space.

Organization

5 My paper is logical and easy to follow.

- My lead gets the reader's attention and goes with the paper.

- Every detail seems to be in the right order.

- My paper follows a pattern that makes sense for this topic.

- It's easy to see how things are connected to my main point.

- My conclusion is just right! Readers will say, "Wow!"

3 Readers can follow this paper most of the time.

- My lead needs to be livelier—but at least it's there!

- Most details are in the right order.

- My paper follows a pattern most of the time.

- Most ideas are connected to my main point. Some aren't, though.

- My conclusion is OK. It's not exciting, but I have one.

1 This paper is hard to follow.

- My paper does not have a lead. I just started writing.

- I wrote ideas as they came into my head. I am not sure the order of details works.

- I don't see any real pattern here.

- I am not sure what my main point is, so it's hard to tell whether my ideas are connected to it.

- I don't really have a conclusion. My paper just stops.

Voice

5 **This paper shows who I am. The reader can tell it's ME!**

- The reader will definitely want to share this aloud with someone.

- I love this topic, so lots of energy comes through.

- I'm writing for my readers, and I want them to love this topic as much as I do.

- This is just the right voice for this topic.

3 **Occasionally this paper shows who I am. The reader can hear ME sometimes. My voice comes and goes.**

- The reader may want to share parts of this paper aloud.

- This was an OK topic, but I couldn't get excited about it.

- I write for my readers some of the time. Other times, I don't think about them at all.

- I think this voice is OK for this topic.

1 **I don't hear much voice in this writing.**

- The reader probably will not want to share this paper aloud.

- This topic bored me, and I sound bored.

- I just wanted this to be over. I do not care much whether anyone reads it.

- My voice does not fit my topic well. It should be stronger or different.

Word Choice

---

5 Every word helps make my writing clear and interesting.

- My verbs have power. They energize my writing.

- My words paint a picture. The reader can tell just what I'm trying to say.

- I got rid of clutter (unnecessary words).

- I used some words that help the reader see, hear, touch, taste, or smell.

---

3 My words are usually clear, but sometimes the reader may really need to concentrate.

- A *few* of my verbs have power. Some could use more muscle.

- The reader can picture what I am talking about if he or she works at it a little.

- I got rid of some clutter, but I missed some, too.

- I thought about helping the reader see, hear, touch, taste, and smell, but sometimes I had trouble doing it.

---

1 My words are hard to understand. I am not always sure what I'm trying to say.

- I am not sure what verbs are. I probably don't have many in my paper.

- It's hard to picture what I am talking about. The writing is out of focus.

- Clutter? I think I might have some. I repeated words and used some words I did not need.

- I did not worry about helping the reader see, hear, touch, taste, or smell. I just used the first words I thought of.

Sentence Fluency

5 My writing is smooth. It sounds natural and is easy to read aloud.

- The reader will love reading this aloud. It is expressive.

- Almost all of my sentences begin in different ways. Some are long, and some are short.

- If I used any dialogue, it sounds like real people talking.

3 Most of my writing is smooth. I might have some choppy sentences or run-ons, though.

- The reader won't stumble reading my paragraph aloud, but it might be hard to read my writing with expression.

- Many of my sentences begin the same way. Their length doesn't vary enough.

- If I used dialogue, it needs some work. Sometimes the people sound real, and sometimes they don't.

1 This is hard to read, even for me! The reader can't tell one sentence from another.

- The reader would have to work hard to read this aloud. I wouldn't want to read it aloud.

- All my sentences are the same. There is no variety at all.

- I tried, but my dialogue doesn't sound like real conversation.

Conventions

5 **A reader would have a hard time finding errors in this paper. It's ready to publish. I should know—I edited it myself.**

- I used conventions correctly to help make the meaning clear.

- I checked the spelling, punctuation, grammar, and capitalization. They are all correct.

- I read this paper silently to myself and aloud, too. I corrected every mistake I saw or heard.

3 **The reader will probably notice some errors. I need to go over this again and look carefully for errors!**

- I did a lot of things right, but I also made some errors. The reader might slow down once or twice because of the errors.

- I checked my spelling, punctuation, grammar, and capitalization. I think they are pretty good. I may have missed a few things, though.

- I did read this paper quickly. I guess I should read it again. I might hear mistakes that my eye missed.

1 **I made so many mistakes that a reader would have a hard time reading this.**

- This paper is so full of errors that it's hard to spot the things I did right.

- I forgot to check a lot of my spelling, punctuation, grammar, and capitalization. I did not really edit this at all.

- I did not read this over to myself. I guess I should. It needs work.

Ideas

5 **The paper has a clear, well-focused main idea and interesting, carefully chosen details that go beyond the obvious to support or expand that main idea.**

- The writer seems to know the topic well and uses his or her knowledge to advantage.

- The main idea is easy to identify and understand. The paper is clearly focused.

- Thoughtfully selected details enhance the main idea and enlighten the reader.

- Filler—unneeded information—has been omitted. Every detail counts.

3 **The paper is clear, but the main idea is not well developed. There are few interesting or relevant details and more information is needed.**

- The writer seems to have a general grasp of the topic.

- The main idea is somewhat clear, or it can be inferred.

- Generalities abound, but little-known, significant, or intriguing details are rare.

- Some information is completely unnecessary.

1 **The writer does not have a clear topic or may need to narrow a topic that is still too broad to handle effectively.**

- The writer displays limited knowledge of the topic.

- The main idea is unclear, and the paper lacks focus.

- Details do not support or expand any larger message.

- Much of the writing simply fills space.

Organization

5 **This writing is logical and easy to follow.**

- The lead grabs the reader's attention and sets the tone for the paper.

- Every detail is in the right place.

- The paper follows an identifiable pattern (chronological order, comparison-contrast, or the like) that suits the topic.

- The reader can easily make connections between details and the writer's main ideas.

- The conclusion is complete. It is neither abrupt nor long-winded.

3 **The reader can follow the direction of the paper most of the time.**

- The paper has a lead, but it does not grab the reader's attention.

- Most details are in the right places.

- A pattern may not be immediately recognizable.

- It is possible to make connections between details and the writer's main idea. Some ideas are irrelevant.

- The paper has a conclusion, though not a particularly strong one.

1 **This paper is hard to follow.**

- There is no lead. The writer just begins the paper.

- Few details are offered.

- It is difficult to identify any pattern within the writing.

- It is difficult to connect details to any main idea or story line; it may be hard to tell what the main point is.

- There is no conclusion. The paper just stops.

Voice

5 **The writing is highly individual. It bears the definite imprint of this writer.**

- The reader will want to share this aloud.

- The writer seems engaged by the topic, and a strong sense of personal energy comes through.

- This writer is writing for a particular audience.

- The voice is appropriate for the audience and topic.

3 **The reader can hear the writer within the piece now and again. The voice comes and goes.**

- The reader might share *moments* aloud, even if he or she does not share the whole piece.

- The writer seems comfortable with the topic but less than enthusiastic. Bursts of energy mix with lulls.

- This writer *could* be writing for a particular audience—or just to get the job done.

- The voice is acceptable for the topic and audience.

1 **It would be difficult to identify this writer. There seems to be no voice in the writing.**

- This piece is not yet ready to be shared aloud.

- The writer sounds bored; perhaps this topic did not work for him or her. It is hard to sense *any* personal engagement.

- The writer is not reaching out to any particular audience.

- This piece lacks voice, or the voice is not suited to the topic. It needs to be stronger or different in tone.

Word Choice

5 **Every word helps make the writing clear and interesting.**

- Strong verbs energize the writing.

- The words paint a vivid picture in the reader's mind. There are many noteworthy words and phrases.

- This writing is free of clutter.

- Sensory words (as appropriate) help readers see, hear, touch, taste, or smell images.

3 **Most words and phrases are clear. Good writing is mixed with vague or misused language.**

- A *few* strong verbs give life to the writing; more are necessary.

- The reader can often picture what the writer is talking about. Some language is either vague or overused.

- Some clutter may make the text wordy in spots.

- The writer misses opportunities to use sensory language.

1 **Word choices are ineffective; they do not help convey the message.**

- The writer does not use strong verbs. The language is flat.

- It's hard to picture what the writer is talking about. Vague or overused language gets in the way.

- The writing may be skimpy, or it may be buried in clutter.

- The writer does not make effective use of sensory language.

Teacher Rubric for

Sentence Fluency

5 **The writing sounds smooth and natural. It is easy to read aloud.**

- This paper can be read aloud with expression.

- Almost all of the sentences begin in different ways. Some are long, and some are short.

- If dialogue is used, it sounds like real conversation.

3 **The writing in this paper is smooth but has a few rough spots. Well-crafted sentences are interspersed with choppy wording or with run-ons.**

- Parts of this paper might be difficult to read aloud smoothly.

- Too many sentences begin the same way, and many sentences are the same length.

- Dialogue, if used, needs some work. Sometimes the language sounds like real conversation, and sometimes it does not.

1 **This paper is hard to read aloud. Sometimes it is hard to tell where one sentence ends and the next one begins.**

- The reader will need to rehearse to read this paper aloud. Some verbal editing will be necessary, too.

- Variety in sentence lengths and beginnings is minimal.

- If dialogue is used, it does not sound like real conversation.

Conventions

5 **The writer is in control of conventions, and this paper is ready to publish.**

- The writer has used conventions correctly, which helps clarify meaning.

- The spelling, capitalization, punctuation, and grammar are, for the most part, correct.

- The writer has read the paper both silently and aloud and has corrected every (or nearly every) mistake.

3 **The writer is somewhat in control of conventions. A careful proofreading will prepare this text for publication.**

- Correct use of conventions enhances meaning in parts of the text. A few errors may catch a reader's eye or slow the reading. Errors do not distort meaning.

- Spelling, capitalization, punctuation, and grammar errors are at an acceptable level and could easily be corrected.

- The writer has read the paper through at least once, but a second reading—silent or oral—could help identify additional errors.

1 **This writer is not yet in control of conventions. Many errors need correcting before this text is ready to publish.**

- Numerous errors slow the reader and occasionally get in the way of the writer's message.

- The text contains many errors in spelling, capitalization, punctuation, and grammar.

- The writer does not appear to have read this paper either silently or aloud. The paper should be edited by the writer and perhaps by an editing partner.

Rationales for the Scores Using the 5-point Rubric

Unit 1: Ideas

Sample Paper 1: *Cafeteria*

Rationale for the Score

Most students should see this paper as **weak.** It received a **2** on the 5-point rubric. It has a main idea: *The cafeteria is disgusting during the lunch hour.* The writer does include some details: the students mixing ketchup and milk or talking with their mouths full. These descriptions create images in the reader's mind. The problem is that we do not have *enough* information for a complete picture. More detail would help. In addition, the writer needs to include more sensory information, such as sounds, smells, and tastes.

Sample Paper 2: *My Cookie Surprise*

Rationale for the Score

Most students should see this paper as **strong.** It received a **5** on the 5-point rubric. The writer paints a clear, vivid picture of an unusual experience, and the images of biting into the hard cookie and using a wad of paper to stop the bleeding are easy to visualize. The writer uses experience and excellent recall of the situation to make the story lively and interesting.

Sample Paper 3: *The Deer Family*

Rationale for the Score

Most students should see this paper as somewhat **weak.** It received a **2** on the 5-point rubric because much more information is needed to make this paper complete. The main idea could be that a deer's lifespan is short because its life is hard. The main idea also might be that the deer is a successful animal species because it has adapted to various conditions throughout the world. The writer makes both points but does not offer enough support for either of them.

Sample Paper 4: *My Most Embarrassing Moment*

Rationale for the Score

Most students should see this paper as **strong.** It received a **5** on the 5-point rubric because it provides a complete story and makes a clear point: *Take time to know what you are doing if you want to avoid embarrassing situations!* More sensory detail and some dialogue would have improved the story.

Unit 2: Organization

Sample Paper 5: *Egypt*

Rationale for the Score

Most students should see this paper as **strong.** It received a **5** on the 5-point rubric because it is easy to follow and moves smoothly from point to point. The lead is striking: *There is more to Egypt than mummies and pyramids.* The conclusion also works well: *Think of a land where having the first and biggest is not that unusual.* The information presented is well organized and the writer connects each point to the main idea without wandering off topic.

Sample Paper 6: *The Embarrassing Play*

Rationale for the Score

Most students should see this paper as **weak.** It received a **2** on the 5-point rubric because the writer wanders enough from the main idea to be confusing. The story begins with the embarrassment of having the little sister go on the stage— but before this idea can be developed at all, the writer introduces a discussion of fashion. The writer returns to the embarrassing moment in the conclusion, but the reader cannot be sure which moment he or she is referring to. The lead shows promise, but the writer does not follow up. The conclusion is ambiguous.

Sample Paper 7: *How to Give a Haircut*

Rationale for the Score

Most students should see this paper as very **strong.** It received a **5** on the 5-point rubric because it is easy to follow, and the writer does not wander from the main topic. The writer includes a step-by-step pattern, though it is also divided into two major sections: what the reader will need for the project and how to do it. In this way, the paper is set up much like a recipe. The lead and conclusion are both strong. The writer starts by explaining that it is not necessary to spend a fortune to get a good haircut—a friend could do it! That's an intriguing introduction, and it sets the paper up well. The conclusion is humorous and effective.

Sample Paper 8: *A New Car*

Rationale for the Score

Though it has a lot of voice and is fun to read, most students should see this paper as **weak.** It received a **2** on the 5-point rubric because it wanders and does not connect key points to any main idea. The story goes from the new family car to the difficulties of coping with a screaming little brother to the challenges of living with a less than brilliant dog to next year's school—and finally back to the car. The lead is rather weak: *Last night my parents bought a new car.* The ending is better: *Oh well, parents are good at some things—like picking out new cars!* Still, neither connects to the writer's main points. This writer really has not settled on any one topic, and this lack is one reason for the paper's weak organization.

Unit 3: Voice

Sample Paper 9: *Accidental Haircut*

Rationale for the Score

Most students should see this paper as **strong.** It received a **5** on the 5-point rubric because it is filled with relevant and lively details. The writer creates vivid impressions—her horror at having the curly comb caught in her hair, her worry that her mother will discover her problem (which she does), and her frenzy over having her hair cut—not to mention the semi-disastrous results. The writer's personality comes through clearly. This is definitely a read-aloud paper.

Sample Paper 10: *Cats Make the Best Pets*

Rationale for the Score

Most students should see this paper as somewhat **weak.** It received a **3** on the 5-point rubric because it is not consistently energetic, even though it has moments of strong voice. The writer seems to genuinely love cats and appreciates the fact that they are independent and easy to care for. This is not a high-energy paper, however. The voice is more sincere and functional than passionate or distinctive.

Sample Paper 11: *Homework Is Important*

Rationale for the Score

Most students should see this paper as **weak.** It has very little energy, and its repetition of key words and ideas is flat and boring. It received a **2** on the 5-point rubric. The writer does not appear particularly engaged, and certainly is writing about a topic that holds little interest for him or her. The generalities that fill the paper—homework is important, homework makes you smart, smart people are interesting—are commonly held beliefs that readers have heard before.

Sample Paper 12: *My Brother the Pain*

Rationale for the Score

Most students should see this paper as **strong.** It is rich with voice—full of humor and energy. It received a **5** on the 5-point rubric. Details enhance the voice, and this is a paper a reader would not mind reading more than once. Even better, the voice is consistent throughout the piece. Some moments may be stronger than others, but the voice never fades.

Unit 4: Word Choice

Sample Paper 13: *Engine*

Rationale for the Score

Most students should see this paper as somewhat **strong.** It received a **4** on the 5-point rubric. Though it could still use revision, it has some good moments, beginning with the very first line: *Vroom! Vroom!* The writer's attempt to reproduce the actual sound of the engine is an example of creative word choice. There are other strong moments, too: *tires screech* and *race out onto the track.* The writer also allows a few tired phrases to creep in, and the paper is in need of some stronger action verbs in places. After a good beginning, the writer relies on modifiers, such as *magnificent,* to wrap things up.

Sample Paper 14: *King of the Surf*

Rationale for the Score

Most students should see this paper as **strong.** It received a **5** on the 5-point rubric. The story could use more sensory detail, yet the verbs (and the general wording and phrasing) are strong. Here are a few examples: *sustain major injuries, sharp implements, hit the wave, paddled out, scouting out, whole ocean flipped, plunged . . . like an anchor, scrunched.* This writer is very selective, and the words paint a clear picture. There is little repetition. The combination of clarity and humor produces strong voice.

Sample Paper 15: *Movies Are My Favorite Thing*

Rationale for the Score

Even though the main idea is clear, most students should see this paper as **weak.** It received a **2** on the 5-point rubric. Words are not misused, but they are certainly overused, for example, *best, huge, really, stuff* appear far too often. These words tell the reader what is happening, but they show the reader little or nothing. Details are also noticeably missing and so are strong verbs. The paper has potential, but the writer needs to describe the sounds and smells of the theater. More sensory detail would greatly improve the paper.

Sample Paper 16: *Life on the Prairie*

Rationale for the Score

Most students should see this paper as fairly **weak.** It received a **2** on the 5-point rubric. Many words are misused, making meaning unclear: *frantic, eradicated, surly* (*surly* stew?), *selective* (*selective* floors?), *abundant, pauperized* (overkill for *poor*). These misused words obscure meaning. The writer does use one strong verb: *eradicated.* Unfortunately, it is not used correctly—since snakes certainly did not *eradicate* the pioneers, and *eradicating* people from their homes does not make sense. This writer is trying hard to breathe some life into the writing, but he or she has simply used too many words incorrectly.

Unit 5: Sentence Fluency

Sample Paper 17: *Alligator*

Rationale for the Score

Most students should see this paper as **weak.** It received a **2** on the 5-point rubric because the sentences are long, rambling, and repetitive. It is difficult to make this paper sound smooth without some rehearsal. With some sentence reconstruction and attention to varied beginnings, this could be a very strong paper. The writer has used some imagination, but the paragraph needs revision.

Sample Paper 18: *Chinese Dragon*

Rationale for the Score

Most students should see this paper as **strong.** It received a **4** on the 5-point rubric. Sentences are varied, the dialogue is believable, and the piece is easy to read. The language is natural, not stilted or phony. Students will have an easy time reading this paper aloud.

Sample Paper 19: *Flying*

Rationale for the Score

Most students should see this paper as **strong.** It received a **5** on the 5-point rubric because virtually all of the sentences begin differently, there are no troublesome fluency problems, and the sentences read smoothly. In addition, the sentences vary in length. The writer does include some fragments, but these enhance the style and voice.

Sample Paper 20: *Shopping*

Rationale for the Score

Most students should see this paper as somewhat **weak.** It received a **2** on the 5-point rubric because the sentences tend to be choppy. Also, many sentences are similar in length, and many have similar beginnings as well. The dialogue between the parents does not emphasize the differences between their approaches to shopping. Some revision of sentence lengths and beginnings will give this paper the fluency it needs.

Unit 6: Conventions

Sample Paper 21: *Flank Steak and Other Treats*

Rationale for the Score

Most students should see this paper as **strong.** It received a **5** on the 5-point rubric because it contains virtually no errors. This writer has done an excellent job of handling conventions effectively and making the text easy to read.

Sample Paper 22: *A Career in Nursing*

Rationale for the Score

Most students should see this paper as **weak.** It received a **1** on the 5-point rubric because it contains many errors. The errors would slow a careful reader.

Sample Paper 23: *The Best Hideout*

Rationale for the Score

Most students should see this paper as somewhat **strong.** It received a **4** on the 5-point rubric because the errors do not impair readability. The errors tend to be small—a missing word, a repeated word, a missing apostrophe, and so on. Most spelling, punctuation, and grammar conventions have been observed. Only moderate editing would be needed to prepare this piece for publication.

Sample Paper 24: *Pizza Mania*

Rationale for the Score

Most students should see this paper as **weak.** It received a **1** on the 5-point rubric because it contains many errors in conventions, making reading difficult. It needs serious editorial review.